The
Canary
Islander

Barrie Mahoney worked as a teacher and head teacher in the south west of England, and then became a school inspector in England and Wales. A new life and career as a newspaper reporter in Spain's Costa Blanca led to him launching and editing an English language newspaper in the Canary Islands. Barrie's books include novels in 'The Prior's Hill Chronicles' series, as well as books for expats in the 'Letters from the Atlantic' series, which give an amusing and reflective view of life abroad.

Barrie writes regular columns for newspapers and magazines in Spain, Portugal, Ireland, Australia, South Africa, Canada, UK and the USA. He also designs websites to promote the Canary Islands and living and working abroad, and is often asked to contribute to radio programmes about expat life.

Visit the author's websites:

http://barriemahoney.com
http://thecanaryislander.com

Other books by Barrie Mahoney

Journeys & Jigsaws (The Canary Islander Publishing) 2013
ISBN: 978-0957544475 (Paperback and eBook)

Threads and Threats (The Canary Islander Publishing) 2013
ISBN: 978-0992767105 (Paperback and eBook)

Letters from the Atlantic (The Canary Islander Publishing) 2013
ISBN: 978-0992767136 (Paperback and eBook)

Living the Dream (The Canary Islander Publishing) 2015
ISBN: 978-0992767198 (Paperback and eBook)

Expat Survival (The Canary Islander Publishing) 2015
ISBN: 978-0992767167 (Paperback and eBook)

Message in a Bottle (The Canary Islander Publishing) 2016
ISBN: 978-0995602700 (Paperback and eBook)

Escape to the Sun (The Canary Islander Publishing) 2016
ISBN: 978-0957544444 (Paperback and eBook)

Expat Voice (The Canary Islander Publishing) 2014
ISBN: 978-0992767174 (Paperback and eBook)

Island in the Sun (The Canary Islander Publishing) 2015
ISBN: 978-0992767181 (Paperback and eBook)

Footprints in the Sand (The Canary Islander Publishing) 2016 ISBN: 978-0995602717 (Paperback and eBook)

Living in Spain
and the Canary Islands

Barrie Mahoney

The Canary Islander Publishing

ISBN 978-0995602724
www.barriemahoney.com

First Published in 2017

The Canary Islander Publishing

Acknowledgements

I would like to thank all those people that I have met on my journey to where I am now.

To supportive friends who helped me to overcome the many problems and frustrations that I faced and taught me much about learning to adapt to a new culture. Also, to friends in the UK, or scattered around the world, who have kept in touch despite being so far away.

To the people that I met whilst working as a newspaper reporter and editor in Spain and the Canary Islands, and for the privilege of sharing their successes and challenges in life.

Disclaimer

This is a book about real people, real places and real events, but names of people and companies have been changed to avoid any embarrassment.

The Canary Islander

DEDICATION

This book is dedicated to people all over the world who dream of a new life, new experiences, new cultures, new opportunities to experience, taste and smell the excitement of a place that is of their own choosing and not merely based upon an accident of birth.

The
Canary
Islander

Contents

Preface

Preface - Living Your Dream

What a year 2017 has been for British immigrants living in Europe, as well as for those hoping to make a new home in the sun. Since I wrote the first 'Letter from the Atlantic' as a newspaper reporter in 2004, so many things have changed. When my partner and I moved to the Costa Blanca, it was a time of great optimism and exciting possibilities. The exchange rate meant that the British living in Europe were getting a very favourable deal. Property prices in Spain were realistic, and for many ordinary people the opportunity of a new life in the sun became a reality and not just a dream.

It was also a time when British entrepreneurs established new and successful businesses in the Costas, and Spain was grateful for the investment and made newcomers welcome. It was a time when it seemed that nothing could halt the enthusiasm of the British for a new life in Spain.

Then there was the financial crash, later to be followed by the EU referendum and what has since become known as 'Brexit'. Looking back, it should have been obvious that the pound was severely over valued for many years, and that many Brits were living in a 'fool's paradise' that would eventually come to an abrupt end. There was rapid devaluation of house prices, leading to negative equity and financial chaos for many who had over extended themselves when buying a property in Spain. A number of British owned businesses in Spain collapsed, leaving many disillusioned and with little option other than to return reluctantly to the country of their birth.

The result of the referendum, initiated by the then Prime Minister, David Cameron, went badly wrong from the point of view of many Brits living in Spain. The result of the referendum was accompanied by a fall in the value of the pound, and left many with a reduction of around 20 per cent of the income that they were used to. Pensioners, and those on a low income were the first to feel the initial impact of the decision to leave the European Union, and for a time it seemed that the rush to leave Britain for a sunnier future had ground to an abrupt halt, as the electorate began to take stock of their new position outside the European Union.

This book, 'Living in Spain and the Canary Islands' began the year with a series of letters that reflected and expressed the mood at the time. Confused as to what the future would bring, there were often angry, and sometimes depressed conversations in bars, restaurants and all areas of British social life in Spain and the Canary Islands, which is where I currently live. Estate agents were gloomy and removal companies were reporting a sudden resurgence in business, as many Brits were leaving Spain and heading back to the UK. Of course, many of the elderly and sick could not do this, because they had neither the resources, good health or inclination to deal with what would be for many a traumatic return to life in the UK. I also doubt that many would survive the rapid drop in temperature either.

The political climate is changing once again. As I look back over these turbulent 12 months, I know that many businesses, banks, estate agents and removal companies in Spain are reporting a greater positivity and enthusiasm from those who are still longing to move from the UK to Europe. For many, the EU referendum has confirmed what they already knew; that they are firstly European and not just British. Politically, many dislike what they see as a new anti-European order within the British political establishment and have decided to vote with their feet.

As well as retirees looking to fulfil their dream of heading for a healthier life in the sun, young people are seeing their future as still being part of the bigger European dream. Despite significant changes, there are new realisations for British people hoping to make a new life within a country of their choosing, and not just the territorial constraints created by an accident of birth.

It is true that many of the opportunities and freedoms have narrowed since myself and many others began our new lives in Spain, as well as other parts of Europe. The opportunities provided by the freedom of movement to live and work in any country across this exciting and inspiring continent are the envy of many across the world and should not be lightly overlooked. Life is short; if you have the enthusiasm and the means, my best advice is to grasp every opportunity to 'live your dream'.

Changing Times

Keep Calm and Carry On!

I received an email from an expat living in Spain's Costa del Sol last week, who was understandably concerned and angry about the falling pound. Basically, he was asking what the UK Government was going to do about it. Apparently, both he and his wife are now having to seriously cut back on both food and entertainment in an effort to save the 300 pounds that they have lost each month due to the fall in the pound-euro exchange rate following Brexit.

On the basis that the pound had fallen in the region of fifteen per cent of its value, at the time of writing, my correspondent must be receiving in excess of 2000 pounds each month to suffer this size of reduction in his income. Although the falling pound is not good news for any expat, I know of many who live on a fraction of that size of income during their retirement years. I am not going to weep too many tears for my correspondent, and merely suggest that he immediately implements a few economy measures.

A drop of this size in income and pensions received from the UK is a serious matter, but many expats tend to overlook the many good years when the strong pound meant being able to live in comparative luxury in Spain, when compared to life in the UK. As in most things in life, there are winners at the expense of losers, and this is a time for readjusting the balance.

I am often told that near exchange rate parity occurred before and certainly during the time of the world economic crisis. It did, and then again, it did not, since the parity exchange rate only applied if you were foolish enough to exchange pounds for euros at some of the rip off currency exchange shops in UK airports.

Most expats that I know, as well as tourists, would never consider doing this, and plan their currency exchange well in advance of their needs, by using one of the more reputable methods of currency exchange. At the time of writing, if you only achieve parity when exchanging pounds for euros, then you clearly haven't done your homework.

Nothing is forever, and all good things have to come to an end sometime. I will no doubt be called a pessimist for my views on Brexit, but I suspect that we are only now catching a glimpse of that rather nasty iceberg that the UK appears to be heading towards, unless more astute minds in the UK Government's current negotiating team intervene with a hefty dose of realism, common sense and a healthy dose of humility.

Will this have any effect upon both intending, as well as already settled expats? There is already some evidence to suggest that many intending expats are putting their plans on hold, particularly if they are intending to purchase a property in Spain, France, Portugal or other European countries.

There is simply far too much uncertainty and volatility at the present time to commit to such a large currency exchange, although this view is contradicted in Spain where there is something of a mini building boom once again in the Costas.

As for expats already living in Europe, the future remains uncertain, and will continue to be in the months ahead. I am reliably informed by several of the larger removal companies who spend much of their time moving Brits to and from Spain and France, that the rate of movement is slower that they first anticipated following the Brexit vote.

This may not come as a surprise to some, since many expats over retirement age could not afford to return to the UK anyway, given the weak pound. Unless retired expats have substantial financial resources, as well as the foresight to retain a property in the UK during their time as expats, housing will be a major and near impossible issue for the returning expat to resolve, particularly since retirement and sheltered housing are in short supply in most regions.

In addition, there are complications concerning the resumption of health care in the UK, and particularly after expats have experienced rather better care in Spain, France and many other European countries that they will receive from an overstretched health service in the UK.

A number of expats that I have spoken to, who have returned to the UK from warmer countries, have told me of serious health issues that they have experienced since returning to a damper and cooler UK climate. The body takes time to adjust to such changes and, quite simply, many older expats simply do not have sufficient time left or the physical ability to cope with such massive adjustments.

During the post Brexit period, despite the many concerns and anxieties, the only sensible thing for many expats to do is to obey that famous instruction on that well-known wartime poster, which is simply 'To Keep Calm, and to Carry On'!

A Glimmer of Hope for Expats in Europe

If you happen to be a determined Brexiter, it is probably better that you do not read this article, since it may lead you to choke on your cornflakes. For those who do value the European ideal and the opportunities that we have been given to live and work in the country of our choice, there is some news that may help to cheer us all up following the recent traumas of Brexit and Trump.

It is already clear that the decision to leave the EU has caused considerable distress and uncertainty for expats, and particularly for those of advanced years and poor health. I know of many who are planning to return to the UK, if their health and finances can stand it, others are claiming citizenship rights from their host countries, whilst others remain in a kind of limbo. Confusion, uncertainty and unnecessary stress is not good for any of us, but it may be that there is a glimmer of hope appearing on the horizon.

Charles Goerens, a member of the Alliance of Liberals and Democrats for Europe Group in the European Parliament representing Luxembourg, is calling for the establishment of European associate citizenship for those who wish to continue to be part of the European project, but are nationals of a former European state.

Simply put, this associate status would give British expats continued rights, such as freedom of movement and the right to reside in member states of the European Union, as well as being able to stand and vote in European elections. In return, associate citizens would pay an annual membership fee directly into the European budget. Those who apply for associate status of the EU would continue to retain their British passports and UK citizenship, which would mean that the status quo would continue, albeit for an annual membership fee.

Charles Goerens makes the point that 48 pcr cent of all British voters wished to remain as European citizens and should continue to have the right to do so. The EU should assist the process in providing a practical solution for UK citizens who are being stripped of their European identity.

Treaty change at European level will be required, since current treaties specify that European citizenship stems directly from national citizenship of member states. European Union citizenship is currently additional to and does not replace national citizenship.

So, what happens next? Nothing substantial can happen until the UK triggers Article 50, which sets the divorce from the EU in motion. Meanwhile, the European Parliament's Constitutional Committee will vote on the amendments, which will be followed by a vote in the European Parliament as early as next year. Further development of the proposals can only take place during the negotiations that follow Article 50 when current treaties will be updated.

Some Brexiters are, of course, unhappy, with the 'Get Britain Out' campaign director complaining that the move will encourage further divisiveness between the British public at a time when unity is required. On the contrary, I think there is little for Brexiters to fear from a move that will offer further democratic choice, and help to protect the rights of those who wish to retain their European identity; one size does not fit all.

Are You Friendly?

This week, I received a very cross email from Dawn, a regular reader of 'Letters from the Atlantic'. Dawn is a British expat who has lived in Italy for many years, and is very unhappy about an article that she recently read in an expat publication. Dawn sent me a copy of the article that was basically a survey of nations that had the most friendly and unfriendly attitudes to expats living in their countries.

The article claimed that Denmark, Switzerland and Norway are the most unfriendly destinations for expats. Despite the generally high quality of life in these countries, they are just not friendly enough with poor attitudes to expats and a local culture that is difficult to get used to.

These 'sinners' were closely followed by Germany and France that ranked 56th and 57th in a list of 67 countries. Again, the general friendliness (or lack of) figured highly in France, whilst in Germany socialising with the locals and the language were major barriers to successful integration. Mind you, it could be worse, with Kuwait, Saudi Arabia and the Czech Republic being the most unfriendly of all.

At the top of the friendliness list are Mexico, Costa Rica and Uganda, with Greece and Cyprus making huge leaps forward in the friendliness stakes. According to the article, these countries bend over backwards to make expats feel at home.

However, the top destinations overall for expats are Taiwan, Malta and Ecuador, which is due to quality of life issues that include financial factors and healthcare, whilst Qatar, Italy and Tanzania plummet to the bottom as the worst countries for expats to live in.

I think that it was at this point that Dawn felt sufficiently moved to fire off an email to me, since she has lived in both France and Italy for a number of years, and resents the implication that both countries are unwelcoming to expats. She makes the point that these countries made her and her partner feel welcome, although initially she found negotiating French bureaucracy a challenge.

However, Dawn also makes the point that being able to speak French helped her to settle during those first few months in a new country. In France, she lived in a small village where she quickly became accepted into the community, whilst in Italy integrating into a large city was more difficult, but Dawn quickly overcame this by helping to support a local animal welfare charity, voluntary work teaching English in her local primary school, as well as helping to deliver bread to elderly local residents from the local bakery!

Dawn's email basically gives all expats a simple lesson in how to be a happy and well integrated expat. Those expats who claim to live in unfriendly countries should ask themselves whether they have bothered to learn the language and take part in local and cultural activities.

Do they appreciate and value local traditions, or attempt to have a conversation with their neighbours? Have they fallen into the usual British expat trap of living in a British enclave, only socialising in British bars and restaurants, complaining about life in their host country and comparing it to the UK through rose tinted glasses? Do they only watch British television and only ever speak in English and expect others to speak to them in English? Frank answers to these questions may give an explanation of why some countries are regarded as more unfriendly than others.

So what about the UK? Based on the data before the Brexit referendum, the UK came in 33rd place in Dawn's article, which was mainly due to friendliness towards expat families, as well as job security. However, the cost of living was thought to be too high, pushing the ranking to a lower position. One can only imagine how expats from Europe view the friendliness of the UK population towards them following the referendum.

Of course, data and statistics can be made, massaged and twisted to interpret almost anything, and surveys such as this are little more than meaningless. As all wise expats like Dawn quickly realise, much of our attitudes about the friendliness of people in our host country is heavily influenced by our attitudes towards them.

Getting Your Hands on a Nice Courgette

I found it difficult to look at a courgette this week; the same goes for broccoli and lettuce too. After all, how could I enjoy such luxuries when I know full well that the good people of the UK cannot get their hands on them? Indeed, according to the UK's favourite tabloid, the Daily Hate, people are craving for them and will pay anything up to ten times the normal price just to get their hands on a nice juicy iceberg.

Indeed, some supermarkets are rationing supplies to prevent 'bulk buying'. The official reason for the shortage is blamed upon poor weather in Spain and other southern European countries, which will probably not be normalised until April. Of course, much depends upon where you shop, and other supermarkets have more than enough stock from other suppliers, although of course this 'shortage' has led to a rapid increase in prices.

It did make me smile when I read on the letters page that some keen Brexiters are complaining that the shortage is a conspiracy by the Spanish, French and other European countries to get their own back on the UK's cheeky attempts to leave the European Union. Apparently, Spanish vegetable growers, who grow around 80 per cent of all EU out of season fresh produce, are so greedy that they prefer to feed their own people courgettes, broccoli and lettuce rather than to send them to the UK where they could get ten times the normal price.

According to the Daily Hate, Spain is accused of "hoarding" fruit and vegetables whilst British shoppers are being rationed. It is just so selfish and typical of those difficult Europeans, isn't it? Well, with the Brexit negotiations about to start, it can only get worse.

Seriously, I am not a great lover of the humble courgette, although I don't mind too much if it is heavily disguised as something else. Indeed, I learned last week that courgettes can now be turned into a kind of spaghetti, which involves the use of an expensive machine to magically turn a courgette into 'courghetti' and, in this way, people will now eat them since they are supremely good for you.

Did you know that all adults should now be eating at least ten portions of fruit and veg each day, rather than five? Apparently, courgettes do the job nicely, resulting in the courgette shortage, as well as increased bowel movement, so please be careful.

Now, broccoli is a different matter; I adore broccoli and particularly when it is served with a nice Stilton or blue cheese sauce. Served with a nice crusty chunk of bread, it is a quick and nutritious meal that I can highly recommend that used to be served as 'Brocco Breath' in one of my favourite UK cafe bars. The name becomes obvious if you use the correct type of strong cheese!

On to the subject of the iceberg lettuce; now be honest, does anyone actually eat and enjoy them? Surely, the main purpose of the iceberg lettuce is to look fresh and lovely when you buy it, to look self-righteous at the check-out when you buy it alongside that pack of jam donuts.

Then it lurks in the back of the fridge unloved and forgotten for a week until it collapses with embarrassment, turning into a pungent brown slurry before it is finally discovered and disposed of; unloved, unused and forgotten. Personally, I wouldn't eat one either; they are tasteless and reminds me of chewing through pages of the Daily Hate, which seriously disables the digestion.

I was surprised to learn that around 90 per cent of fruit consumed in Britain is imported from Europe, as well as around 50 per cent of vegetables. The UK also has to import significant quantities of fruit and vegetables from South America and the US, which makes a nonsense of the carbon footprint, as well as the UK economy.

I was faced with boxes of fresh courgettes, broccoli and the dreaded iceberg lettuce in my local supermarket in the Canary Islands this week. The prices were about normal for this time of the year, and until I read the article I was unaware of what the fuss is all about.

If you are really desperate for an iceberg lettuce, courgette or broccoli, might I suggest that you pop out with an empty suitcase and take advantage of our plentiful supplies of fruit and vegetables, as well as our sunshine. Alternatively, there are always frozen food products.

A Poisonous Debate

I read a story this week about a woman who left her husband of twenty-two years, reportedly because he voted for Donald Trump and she felt a sense of acute betrayal that affected all areas of their relationship. This story also raises some poignant issues in relation to Brexit and other current issues where the original intention of a well-considered, thoughtful and civilised debate has turned into a poisonous one affecting many areas of national, as well as everyday life and relationships.

Burning passions on both sides of the debate concerning the Trump and Brexit debates have taken their toll upon many families and friendships, and continue to do so.

During the run up to the EU referendum, I received several very unpleasant emails from some expats criticising my views on remaining in the European Union that I expressed in 'Letters from the Atlantic'. Yes, I am a committed Remainer, and an unashamedly committed European for as long as I can remember.

What surprised me at the time was not only the strength of feeling expressed, but that the criticisms were coming from expats who were themselves living in EU countries. I wondered then, as I do now, how it is possible to be an expat living in Europe, and enjoying its many advantages, yet wanting to deny these advantages to others. It is an example of what seems logical to some is completely illogical to others.

As a democrat, I reluctantly accepted the result of the referendum, but I do reserve the right alongside the 48%, who lost the argument, to object, to complain, to challenge and to criticise where appropriate as the UK staggers towards an eventual agreement with the European Union.

The Leave campaign had a 52% win, and it is important to respect the views of the majority, which in most cases will have been carefully considered; however, the views of the minority should not be ignored.

A further reminder of the American woman who has left her husband because he had voted for Trump arrived in my email inbox this morning. I was sad to receive a message from one of my regular correspondents telling me that he and his partner have decided to separate after several years of living together, mainly because of their differences over the EU referendum.

Apparently, their views were not reconcilable and since on one occasion, it turned to violence, the couple decided to call it a day. I suspect, and hope, that the referendum was not the only reason for the break-up of this relationship, but it does help to explain the differences and strength of feelings involved.

One thing that struck me most in this email was the comment, which was similar to the experiences of the American woman, that my correspondent felt betrayed by his partner, whom he had trusted implicitly for many years.

I have read about and am aware of a number of families and friends that are having problems coming to some kind of reconciliation over this controversial issue, which I initially found difficult to understand. If I am honest, my own attitudes to some people that have forcibly expressed a very different view to my own has changed my perceptions of them, and which I am sure, has changed their perceptions of me.

In most cases, it is not sufficient to end a friendship, but does make me more cautious in what I say about a number of issues; in other words, the openness and mutual trust has gone, at least for the time being.

Well, the genie is now well and truly out of the bottle and it is true that many people now feel liberated to say exactly what they feel about immigration, inequality, foreigners, governments, as well as a host of many other grievances that appear to have been suppressed for many years. If these views are expressed clearly, calmly and without malice, it can be a good thing, yet from what we have seen in the mainstream media, as well as in social media, in recent weeks, I somehow doubt it.

What's Not to Like?

Although the current 'party line' in the UK appears to demand that the European Union be viewed with acute suspicion and blamed for everything that has gone wrong in Europe and, in particular, the United Kingdom, there are still many of us that actually appreciate the EU and all that it has achieved over the years.

So, before any determined Brexiters reading this article choke on their cornflakes, I should add a rider that I am viewing its achievements through the eyes of an expat living in Spain and the Canary Islands. The UK has made its own decision and it is time to move on.

The EU's anniversary summit and celebrations are due to take place on 25 March 2017, and although the British Prime Minister has been invited, at the time of writing it is anticipated that she will not attend on the basis that it is not regarded as appropriate for the UK to take part in an act of unity and forward planning when the country is about to leave.

On this day, EU leaders will gather in Rome to look back over 60 years when just six countries embarked on a project aimed at uniting Europe. The Treaty of Rome was signed on 25 March 1957 by the then leaders of France, Germany, Italy, Belgium, the Netherlands and Luxembourg.

As well as a time for celebration, it will be a time for reflection, as well as looking forward to a challenging new decade that will see the UK leave the EU, as well as a new and unpredictable US President to deal with.

In Spain and the Canary Islands, the post Franco period could have been one of acute turmoil and political unrest, but the EU nurtured this troubled country into the successful and peaceful democracy that we see today. I am not saying that Spain could not have done this on its own, but it would have been much harder and a more painful process to achieve in so short a space of time.

Much of the island where I live, half of which was mostly a barren desert wilderness sixty years ago, has been transformed into an island holiday paradise where many holidaymakers come to escape to the sun. Major infrastructure projects, such as roads, bridges, and tunnels cut though mountain regions have been funded by the European Union enabling all of the island to be developed, which benefits residents and tourists alike. Again, without this level of funding, I doubt that this development would have happened.

As far as benefiting my own life, and for many others like me, the freedom to live and work in any of the member states has been one of the most significant benefits, accompanied by the freedom to purchase property, open a business and enjoy life in a country of my own choosing, rather than being trapped in the country of my birth.

For me, this has been a blessing that will be denied to others through rigid immigration policies and other restrictions that have become the narrative of many in the UK.

Citizens' confidence in the EU has been badly shaken in recent times due to the World Economic crisis, the clumsy handling of debt for countries, such as Greece, and the migrants' crisis.

During this period of doom and gloom, it is easy to forget the EU's many achievements, which include 57 per cent of all UK trade, clean rivers and beaches, structural support for areas of decline such as Wales, Cornwall and Lincolnshire, cleaner air, recycling, cheaper mobile phone charges, cheaper air travel, no paperwork or customs between member countries, access to European health services, EU funded research, labour protection, maternity rights, counter terrorism… I could go on for a few more pages, but you get the general idea? Above all, after centuries of war between European neighbours, the EU has finally brought peace.

I, for one, will be celebrating the European Union and the influence for good that it has upon Spain and the Canary Islands, as well as for the people of Europe on 25 March. As with so many things in our fast-moving lives, we often do not know the value of something until we have lost it.

No Smiling Please, We're British!

I'm sure that we have all heard of the British 'Stiff Upper Lip', but until recent experiences when attempting to renew my passport I was always unclear as to what this expression really meant. Have you tried practicing one in front of the mirror recently? It really is very difficult.

Over the years, I have received emails from expats telling me of some of their experiences and problems when renewing British passports. It all used to be relatively easy for expats.

Usually, popping into the local Consulate office, handing over the usual batch of forms, a couple of photos and the fee, and the passports were either processed internally, sent to the British Embassy or to the UK for processing. It usually didn't take too long and there was often very little fuss and bother. The system worked, although it sometimes creaked a little during seasonal peaks of heavy demand.

Then there was terrorism, requirements for additional security, biometric passports... and then there was Belfast. Now, don't get me wrong, I am sure that the staff in the Belfast passport office are a splendid bunch of people, and I am sure that they don't mind a spot of good natured criticism from time to time.

Frankly, it seems there are a few staff tucked away in the bowels of the Belfast office who could be best described as 'Jobsworths'. According to several of my correspondents, passport applications and renewals have been delayed, returned or refused simply because "your photo did not meet requirements".

We all know that getting a passport photo can be a life or death situation - we just have to get it right, don't we? What do I wear? Is the hair ok? What about the smile? Am I slouching on the kiosk stool? Which is my best side?

After all, the passport photo will live with us for around ten years and will determine whether or not we will be treated decently as one of Her Majesty's esteemed subjects or thrown into a grubby jail in a foreign country. The passport and accompanying photo are essential and valuable, and make us real people if we wish to travel.

Last week, it was my turn. Instead of popping my passport renewal application into the local Consulate office for it to be processed and returned from Madrid, I am now told that in the interests of customer service and increased security it will now be quicker and simpler for me to apply online, and then send the application to Belfast for it to be returned by courier four weeks later, if I am fortunate.

All this for the princely sum of £102 with an incredible range of valuable consular services thrown in as well. What's not to like? Bargain at half the price.

Several correspondents have told me that passport applicants should be very careful not to use the passport photo kiosks that are readily available in most of Spain, because they do not provide photos of the size specified by the UK's passport office.

It was with this warning in mind that I called into a photographic shop to ask if they could provide me with a set of passport photos. The very helpful lady in the shop immediately asked if it was for a British passport. If so, I would have to be very careful as smiling is strictly forbidden. Apparently, applicants from France, Spain, Germany and Ireland are free to smile like Cheshire cats if they wish, but British applicants must look stony-faced into the camera.

It took the photographer four attempts before she was satisfied that my photo would be acceptable. Apparently, I looked far too cheerful, and so for the final attempt I used my best 'cross face', which I usually reserved for naughty children behaving badly in the playground. Eventually, the photographer was content that my photos would pass the UK test and I was sent on my way.

I have now completed my application form and it is ready to post. Whether or not the Passport Office in Belfast will let me have a new passport after reading this article remains to be seen. I also have a hideous passport photo that will only ever be shown to the poor souls checking me in at airport security. My best advice for fellow passport applicants? Just aim for the British 'Stiff Upper Lip', and you will be fine.

Even More Ashamed to be British

April Fool's week has been an interesting one for dedicated expats living in Europe. Firstly, we had all the fun, games and drama surrounding THAT letter written by the Prime Minister, delivered by a grinning, bearded Cheshire Cat of a diplomat clutching a smart, new briefcase, to poor Mr Tusk representing the European Commission.

Am I the only one wondering why Teresa May didn't simply send an email, or that all time Spanish favourite, the Blessed Fax instead? No, we had to have quill and ink and probably a seal, and possibly written on vellum. I know the Brits are into tradition in a big way, but this was all really rather silly, wasn't it? All these festivities were accompanied by the banshee calls of Brexiters shrilly proclaiming their usual cries of jubilation, "We won, get over it!" No, I think not.

We then had all that Gibraltar nonsense and the threat made by an elderly ex-leader of the Tory Party, suggesting the possibility of war with Spain. Really? Now that makes huge sense considering that both the UK and Spain are joint, loyal members of NATO, and usually the best of friends. Still, the fact that he was rather quickly demoted to 'ex-leader of the Tory Party' should tell us all rather a lot about his dubious diplomatic skills, as well as his mental stability.

May I kindly suggest that he would be far better off sucking wine gums in a home for the elderly rather than trotting around TV studios spreading his message of hate about our friends and neighbours?

Maybe the House of Lords, which is the UK's most expensive retirement home, is the more appropriate place for him after all?

I mustn't forget the mind-blowing revelation of the British plan to blow up the Channel Tunnel with a nuclear bomb, if the neighbours don't play nicely, which also popped up in the UK press this week. Nice one guys, but maybe it could cause a bit of a problem for the good people living in Dover who, I suspect, would not be too keen on the idea, since it could blow a significant part of the south coast to pieces.

After all, nuclear bombs do tend to create a bit of a mess, which could be awkward since the UK relies on the French for quite a lot of electricity nowadays. The fact that it was ever even considered as a disruption tactic many years ago should tell us a great deal about the British anti-European psyche. Fortunately, both the Spanish and French have a good sense of humour and none of this abuse appears to have been taken too seriously. "Calm down, dears", was the predictable response from the Spanish - sensible people.

The crowning glory in the British press this week was that brain numbing headline in the Sun proudly proclaiming "Up Yours Senors!" (which should really be Señors, but maybe I am being a tad pedantic) that encapsulated the Sun's thoughtful message to Spain and the European Union, together with the less well-considered sub heading of "Our Message to the Meddling Leaders of Spain and the EU".

Unfortunately, the message was rather lost alongside advertisements for holidays in the sun, (let's all have holidays in Blackpool and not Benidorm nowadays, folks) but the thought was there, however inarticulately expressed.

On a more serious note, I am more or less old enough to remember the protestation of France's then President Charles de Gaulle who was horrified about the possibility of the United Kingdom joining the European project. "Non, non, non" was his entirely reasonable response to Britain's applications to join. Of course, he was right; he knew only too well then, which many thinking expats have known for many years, that Britain was never suited to joining the EU in the first place.

The British island mentality, with its mistaken nostalgia for a past, and not particularly glorious, Empire still haunts the British psyche today. "Be careful what you wish for" is an expression that I have been continually reminded of since the referendum, and which seemed even more relevant this week.

I don't think I have ever been quite so ashamed to be British as I have been this week, and I look longingly at those who are blessed to have Irish, Spanish, German or Swedish passports. Looking back, many of the issues that are currently surfacing have been simmering for many years.

On a more positive note, despite the dire warnings of fervent Brexiters who are willing the EU to collapse, I firmly believe that the EU will become even more united and stronger without the UK in the years ahead; I certainly hope so.

Meanwhile, I have been tempted to join a number of organisations on Facebook this week. Although I agree with one called 'Campaign for a Fair Deal', I am forced to admit that this view remains beyond my understanding, or my willingness to submit to.

Personally, I am still grieving and not yet ready for any kind of deal outside Europe, let alone a fair one. Still, I'll keep taking the pills and maybe one day I'll get over it. Meanwhile, if there any good Europeans out there, who would like to adopt quite a few disillusioned Brits, please let me know.

Inflationary Gin

It is strange how fashion works, with what is 'in' and what is 'out' endlessly changing on what often seems like a whim. However, one piece of news took my attention this week; news that many expats will not be surprised to read.

I have quite a lot of time for Mark Carney, that earnest, Canadian banker who currently presides over the Bank of England as its governor. It is true that before, during and following the Brexit referendum, Mr Carney had a turbulent time. Accused of being too pessimistic in his forecasts by some during the EU referendum, with the more outspoken of his critics calling for his resignation.

Still, he has remained calm under fire and even managed to oversee the release of that rather lovely new one pound coin. With a bit of luck, he should remain happily in his post for the next few years.

I like the Governor's grounded, and clearly spoken approach. I have previously felt that his predecessors would either drop off to sleep mid interview, or send me into a comatose state when listening, but the present Governor does seem to have his eye on the ball. However, I do feel that he would do well to take a little advice from the hordes of gin drinkers, both at home and abroad. Yes, gin is most certainly 'in'.

We hear quite a lot about inflation and discussions about whether interest rates will rise or fall, which can be very boring. I am very concerned that Mr

Carney currently fails to mention the price of gin when debating these very serious inflation forecasts.

According to experts on the subject, the price of gin can seriously affect inflation statistics, so much so that the Office of National Statistics will shortly include the nation's favourite tipple in the 'typical shopping basket' that is used to calculate inflation. Gin has been added because sales of it have boomed in recent times, which I am told is because of the 40 or so new distilleries that have opened since 2016, as well as effective, persuasive marketing.

Reportedly, gin has been HM Queen Elizabeth's favourite tipple for many years. The British public has followed her lead, and drunk more gin than ever in recent years, notching up a 16 per cent increase in sales that has now reached an impressive £1 billion. Some experts claim that gin is needed to smooth the way, as well as easing the pain, as the country heads towards Brexit.

Although gin has been a popular member of the British drinks cabinet for many years, it was nowhere near as popular as other spirits, such as vodka that used to be the main choice of alcohol in nightclubs. It seems that vodka has now fallen out of fashion, and gin has taken its place. Of course, this is not news to the thousands of expats who have cherished G&Ts on their sun terraces for many years, and has become a staple part of their liquid diet.

As far as that eternal 'shopping basket' is concerned, I was saddened to read that brake pads, along with menthol cigarettes and non-smartphone handsets have now been removed. I would have thought that decent brakes were essential in light of all of that gin flowing around the country.

I should stress that the UK's newly revised 'shopping basket' will not only consist of gin, but that children's scooters, cycle helmets, cough syrup and half-chocolate-coated biscuits will now also be added. The logic of the 'shopping basket' escapes me, but I am sure that that nice Mr Carney will find it all very helpful. As for gin, personally I cannot stand the stuff, but I am always happy to defend the virtues of a nice bottle of malt.

Taking the 'Brit' Out of Britain

Like many expats, I completed and posted my voting form for the UK General Election yesterday. In some ways, it was a significant moment, and I should have taken a photo of the event, since this may be the last time that my partner and I will be allowed to vote as expats living in Spain. We will soon hit the 15-year rule that applies to expats, after which we are no longer eligible to vote under current UK rules.

There has been pressure, including court action, over many years to force the UK Government to change the 15-year rule for expats to one where expats may vote for life, but this has always been thwarted, delayed and convenient reasons given for not proceeding. I guess much depends upon the way that the governing party views expat votes; are we likely to support the current Government or not?

Despite the shortcomings of the current electoral system, which fails to represent the views of a wider constituency through proportional representation, we should always take the opportunity to use our vote. There are some expats who claim that expat voting is a pointless exercise and even morally wrong, since we no longer live in the country, do not claim benefits, and do not use the health service.

Many expats rarely visit the UK after they have left, and only return for the occasional family wedding or funeral, so they question whether they have the right to express an opinion that can seriously affect the conditions of the population remaining in the UK.

Expats do have a right to express an opinion as to who should form the next UK Government. Many expats have children and elderly relatives living in the UK, and feel the need to have even a minor involvement in the future direction of the country. The old saying that "You can take the Brit out of Britain, but you cannot take Britain out of the Brit' is so true in these circumstances.

Many UK expats receive a pension of some kind from the UK. The level and conditions linked to receipt of the UK state pension or company pension, and the amount received, is determined by government policies. Exchange rates and currency fluctuations are also the direct result of government policies that form the economic health of the nation.

The levels of state benefits, even winter fuel payments to British expats residing in some of the colder European countries, and reciprocal health services are all determined by the UK government of the day.

Many expats continue to pay taxes to the UK government, based on UK earnings and pensions even though they left the UK many years ago. It is therefore right that expats should continue to express a view as to who should spend their taxes and on what priorities.

The electoral system in the UK is by no means perfect, since it fails to represent the wider range of views of a complicated and increasingly vocal population. We are told that the current 'first past the post system' continues to have many advocates, but in recent years it has not served us well, and many voters feel disillusioned and disenfranchised by most politicians.

The opportunity to change the voting system was put to a referendum vote several years ago, and rejected by voters, and so we have to make the best of what we have.

Expat votes are now even more important since the UK is about to leave the European Union, where relationships, deals and agreements with our host countries will become even more important in the years ahead.

We may feel that a simple cross against the name of a person that we do not know, and support for a political party that will eventually let us down is a pointless exercise, but it is all that we have and it is right to use it.

I hope that whichever political party eventually forms a government, they will recognise the need to ensure that British expats can continue to exercise this simple democratic right to be involved. The 15-year rule should be abolished and expats should be allowed to vote for life.

Fiestas, Superstitions and Plots

The
Canary
Islander

The Evils of Apple Bobbing

Halloween is over for another year, thank goodness. At risk of sounding both a prude and a party pooper, this is one of the annual rituals that I detest with a vengeance. Don't get me wrong, I enjoy a good party as much as the next person, but this tacky, heavily commercialised celebration of evil is, for me, a step too far. Also, I don't think it is too unreasonable to refuse to answer the doorbell when 'trick or treaters' come calling after 10.00pm.

It wasn't always like this. When we first moved to Spain and the Canary Islands, Halloween was virtually unknown, with the main event being the following day, All Saints Day, when it was customary to visit the graves of dead relatives, with family members often picnicking in the cemetery.

In some ways, it all seemed a little macabre to British sensitivities about death, but we all remember the departed in different ways and this was an example of the Spanish way of doing things at that time.

In the last ten years or so we have seen the American way of 'celebrating' Halloween, together with the expensive commercialism of an event that used to be little more than a hollowed-out pumpkin fitted with a candle; indeed, Halloween 'trick or treats' were never part of Spanish culture.

It has moved from being a spooky night for the kids to enjoy to one where 'trick or treat' is seen as a serious and often threatening event for adults to enjoy as a preliminary to a nightmarish party at a local bar until the middle hours of the morning. Indulging in 'blood curdling' cocktails whilst trying not to look too embarrassed in a ridiculous costume, I doubt that many of the departed are remembered much before mid-afternoon on All Saints Day, and that is if the headache allows. As for a cemetery picnic, let's forget it.

Looking back to my career as teacher, I remember the excitement of Halloween when children made and drew witches, black cats and cauldrons. They enjoyed making and chanting spells, writing spooky poems and stories, but that is usually as far as it went, although I do remember one painful exception.

As a young and newly appointed head teacher, I shall never forget one unfortunate Halloween when I was expected to attend an afternoon meeting at County Hall. Later that evening, I received an animated, irritable phone call from the Chair of Governors, who was the village vicar, advising me that he had received a serious complaint about my management of the school.

Bewildered by his opening criticisms, I asked for more details and was informed by this humourless and pompous man that a parent had called him to complain that staff were indulging in witchcraft and evil practices and that, as a church school, we should know better. I listened and assured my caller that I would give it my full attention the following day.

Chatting to staff over coffee at break time the following morning, it became clear that my infant teacher, a well-meaning but generally incompetent soul, had decided to let her class have a Halloween party in my absence. From what I could gather, this involved drawing, face painting and making witches' hats, chanting spells and apple bobbing, which I was surprised to learn that all witches worthy of a black cat and broomstick were expected to indulge in from time to time. It wasn't even mentioned on the curriculum planning sheets for the week, and I suspect that good, last minute intentions had all got a little out of hand.

Despite this, my loyal and perceptive school secretary, who always took it upon herself to prowl around the school in my absence, assured me that nothing untoward had been going on, and that the children had enjoyed themselves, albeit noisily, but adding that the caretaker was not too happy when she arrived to clean the classroom.

Later that afternoon, I met the parents who had made the complaint. They appeared to be a decent young couple who had recently converted to become fundamental Baptists. As with most religions, it is often the newly converted who are the most extreme and they were clearly unhappy that the school entertained any kind of celebration of Halloween.

We talked about the issue at some length and eventually the couple agreed that they had over reacted, but would prefer that their son didn't indulge in the evils of apple bobbing ever again. I agreed to their terms, and in return the couple agreed to run a fundraising stall at the forthcoming Christmas Fair.

As it turned out, this young couple became the most supportive and dedicated fundraisers of all the parents that I ever came in contact with. However, I was never able to face the idea of apple bobbing ever again, and I continue to treat Halloween with great suspicion.

"Put the Kettle On"

During these gloomy, cold, winter days of the post Brexit referendum, when the anointing of Donald Trump as the new leader of Western democracy confirms for many that the world is going quietly mad, there is one thing certain to cheer us up - 'a nice cup of tea'.

Those of a certain age will know just how important tea is to the psyche and general well-being of most Brits. Most of us were weaned on the stuff and it runs through our veins in copious amounts. It is what makes Britain great; it is the stuff of Empire, Winston Churchill, Shakespeare, Harry Potter, Hugh Grant and cream teas. Indeed, it is a well-known truism that you are not a real Brit unless you drink at least ten cups of the stuff each day. Any less than this and you are regarded as a fraud and imposter, or maybe even a European, no argument.

During those damp, cold days in the UK, many of us would feel warmed and comforted by 'a nice cup of tea'. During a crisis, or during those times when it is difficult to know what to say to someone who is ill or in distress, the usual British response is to "put the kettle on". I suspect that it is one of the few things that unite the people of Britain; forget the Union flag, just bring out the Tetley's!

There is, of course, the added advantage that as the temperature drops, you might find yourself reaching for 'a nice cup of tea', because of the obvious benefits of warming your hands around the cup and temporarily banishing the cold. Recent studies reveal that there is a basic psychological factor when drinking 'a nice cup of tea'. It makes us feel warm and friendly towards others.

In one experiment, people were asked to rate strangers on how welcoming and trustworthy they thought they were. Holding 'a nice cup of tea' made them rate the strangers higher on these attributes, whilst holding a cold drink had the opposite effect. Expats should note from this experiment that holding a chilled glass of sangria when meeting strangers is not always such a good idea unless they have carefully thought about the possible dire consequences that may follow such an encounter.

In the study, it was found that those holding hot drinks, such as a 'nice cup of tea', were more likely to be generous, and less likely to display behaviour considered to be selfish. Apparently, this is due to strong linguistic and metaphorical links created in the brain by repeatedly using the words 'warm' or 'cold' to describe personalities.

Several years ago, I was involved in a survey for an expat newspaper that focussed on what items Brits miss most when living in another country. Top of the list was 'a nice cup of tea', closely followed by a range of other items, such as pork pies and baked beans. Although I was initially taken aback about the vehemence with which 'foreign tea' was criticised, I was not surprised, because I shared the general opinion expressed.

The general consensus seems to be that it is almost impossible to get a decent cup of tea in continental

Europe. I know of many expats who make a special point of bringing back teabags from the UK whenever they visit, or ask friends and relatives to bring some out for them.

The fact that most of the popular brands of tea are readily available from supermarkets in Europe goes unnoticed, with the fanatical claims that "Yorkshire Tea is the best in the world", when to others it tastes exactly like all other brands available in continental Europe, which I am sorry to say is to me very similar to lukewarm dishwater.

Of course, real tea drinkers complain about the quality of the water in Europe; they will insist upon using only bottled water and certainly never water from the tap. Others complain about the temperature that the water is heated to, forgetting that a kettle is a kettle whether it is bought in Blackpool or Benidorm.

Tea aficionados will complain about 'a nice cup of tea' being served in a glass cup rather than one of the bone china variety, an unforgivable error in Europe, but forgetting the dubious quality of the chipped mugs that are in common use in cafes all across the UK. Others will complain about the flavour of milk (if added), the quality of the sugar (if used) and indeed whether or not higher temperatures have destroyed the flavour of the tea in the packet before it is even purchased.

Personally, I have come to the view that it is nothing to do with the quality of tea, water, cups or the temperature of the water, but simply because it is European, and this is the real reason behind the Brexit referendum. If the UK Government had appointed a Minister for Tea Drinking long ago, much of the Brexit discussions could have been avoided.

In any case, the availability and quality of 'a nice cup of tea' in Europe will continue be considered and discussed long after the Brexit negotiations are completed; after all, it is simply a question of priorities in life.

As for me, I gave up being a tea drinker almost immediately upon arrival in Spain, as I could not bear to ruin my tea drinking palate, which I now reserve for special and rare occasions, such as a National Trust cream tea during occasional visits to the UK. At a time of crisis, I resort to a nice cup of green tea, but nowadays I am a confirmed coffee drinker. Maybe I have now formally ceased to be British.

Carnival Time in the Canary Islands

Christmas, New Year and Three Kings Day are all over at last, as is Blue Monday (16 January), which is the most depressing day of the year, according to a happy band of media reporters. It is now time to shake away those winter blues, search out a fabulous costume and get ready for Carnival – Canaries style!

Carnival has been celebrated across the Canary Islands since 1556 just before the Christian period called Lent, forty days before Easter, and often around Shrove Tuesday or Mardi Gras.

Lent previously meant that Christians gave up eating meat, so just before this forty-day period the Canary Islanders were determined to take the term 'party' or fiesta to a higher level, which normally involves locals dressing up in fabulous costumes, when often men become women and women become men, just for the fun of it, and of course to have your photo taken.

The dates of Easter change each year and so the date of Carnival across the Canary Islands also changes, so that although the capital cities of each of the Canary Islands have the biggest parades and open-air entertainment, many smaller towns also hold their own Carnival parades.

These parades have large floats that carry many in amazing costumes who often throw sweets or even offer those watching small cups of Canarian rum.

Before the big parades there are also competitions for the best Carnival Queen (ladies), Carnival Dame (older ladies), Carnival Junior Queen (young girls) and of course the best Drag Queen (guess)!

There are also singing competitions called Murgas, when local people on each island sing songs that can often be very rude to those living on other islands.

Carnival starts when a large sardine appears, and it ends when the sardine is taken out to sea, where it dies, and many spectators will be seen crying! It is an emotional and passionate event, often reflecting the partying frolics of the previous night!

Expat residents and tourists that visit during this Carnival period should make sure that they join in the party and learn more about local customs and traditions. There are many shops near tourist areas that sell good value Carnival costumes, so there is no reason why foreigners cannot join in the Canary Islanders' celebrations.

Most municipalities have colourful posters that advertise the local events of Carnival, but some places tend to think that Carnival only involves local people, and they will already know when and where to go.

The information shown on The Canary Islander website give dates and times for Carnival events in all the Canary Islands, but it is a good idea to check with local Tourist Information Offices too.

Take plenty of photos and selfies, because the rich cultural mix of Canary Islanders have strong connections with South America, Cuba and other Caribbean islands, which means that when Carnival comes to the Canary Islands it challenges the Carnival in Rio de Janeiro, and some think it is even better!

One word of warning for those visiting Santa Cruz in La Palma for Carnival! The locals also celebrate White Monday (the day before Shrove Tuesday), when locals only wear white clothes, and then after a certain signal, throw white talcum powder over everyone.

Los Indianos celebrates Canary Islanders who were previously transported to Spanish colonies, and returned when they had become successful. So there is a point to White Monday, but the talcum powder goes everywhere, and those with breathing problems should watch from a distance, as the powder storm spreads quickly and is not the healthiest substance to breathe in.

Las Palmas in Gran Canaria also celebrates White Monday in the old streets of Triana and Vegueta, with special permission of the islanders of La Palma.

Carnivals in Las Palmas de Gran Canaria and Santa Cruz de Tenerife are often billed as "Second Only to Rio", so if you really would like to take part in a huge, crazy, frivolous spectacle of colour and vitality, make sure you don't miss it!

When is a Pirate Not a Pirate?

Many commentators will agree that since the vote for the UK to leave the European Union, the views of the general population have become increasingly fractious and divided in attitudes towards 'foreigners'. Nothing is new, and the British have always been suspicious of their European neighbours.

The Daily Mail, Express, Sun and, indeed, Facebook and Twitter are all currently having a field day in distorting 'the truth', whatever that may be. By now, we should all have begun to realise that there is no such thing as 'the truth', which, at best, is merely a perception of how we interpret an event, based upon our base opinions and prejudices. 'The truth' is always open to manipulation and distortion by others, however well meaning.

Do you remember any of your school history lessons? I certainly remember exciting historical events that I was taught as a pupil at school, as well as the content of lessons that I taught as a teacher. Was Cromwell a revolutionary hero, or was he a genocidal war criminal? I guess much of the answer will depend upon whether or not you hold an Irish passport.

What about Sir Francis Drake, Sir Walter Raleigh, whilst not forgetting Admiral Nelson's attack on Tenerife? Were they simply well-meaning explorers and adventurers seeking to enhance the common good, or profiteers, warmongers and unpleasant pirates?

We often like to label people from the past as saints or sinners, but much depends upon what you have been taught to believe, as well as which country you have been taught in. For me, the definition of a pirate has certainly changed since I moved to Spain and the Canary Islands.

A report from the University of Las Palmas in Gran Canaria, which is undertaking an archaeological study in Fuerteventura to locate the remains of an estimated 90 English pirates, took my eye this week. These English pirates died during a battle in the Eighteenth Century with the residents of the Canary island of Fuerteventura. It is an interesting story, so let us turn the clock back 277 years to the year 1740...

The 'War of Jenkins' was a conflict that lasted from 1739 to 1748 between Spain and England, which refers to the ear of an English pirate captain that was cut off. In 1740, English pirates launched two major attacks on Fuerteventura, with a month between them.

The Fuerteventura militia were successful in both of these pirate attacks, which also demonstrates the lack of harmony between England and Spain at this time.

The first attack involved 50 English pirates looting a village, whilst failing to realise that the island militia had already been placed in defensive positions. Towers at strategic locations had been built to watch out for English pirates who often attacked this island.

Thirty English pirates were killed and 20 were taken prisoner. Islanders attacked the English invaders with clubs and stones, and hid behind a wall of camels when they fired muskets at them. These English prisoners were shipped off to the island of Tenerife to be dealt with.

A second English pirate attack took place one month later, but the number of pirates is disputed, as some reports claim that between 200 and 300 pirates were involved, whilst another suggests that fifty English pirates were killed. The second attack was put down with much greater brutality; no prisoners were taken alive and all the English pirates were killed.

The Fuerteventura islanders showed no mercy after this second audacious attack. This new research will last for several years, and whilst focussing on the conflict, will also search for the remains of the English pirates who were killed in Fuerteventura.

We often refer to Viking pirates raping and pillaging the British Isles, but sometimes I guess we should look closer to home for unreasonable behaviour. When we next visit a museum to admire Spanish gold, trinkets, doubloons and other treasures, let us remember that these were often stolen by English pirates from our European neighbours. Let's face it, we have always had suspicions about anyone living across the water.

Who Loves a Party?

Newly arrived expats living in Spain and the Canary Islands will quickly learn that expat lives are punctuated with fiestas to celebrate the life of a particular saint or a special period in Spanish and Canarian history. Despite the irritation that fiestas can creep up on the unsuspecting expat, ruining plans to go shopping or to visit the bank, they are an intrinsic part of Spanish life and the wise expat soon learns to join in with the moment.

Initially, many expats think that the day of the fiesta is when it all happens. This is a big mistake and new expats quickly learn that fiestas actually begin during the late afternoon and evening on the day before. This is sensible, because it leaves plenty of time to dress up, do the cooking and to gather family and friends together before the actual event.

In reality of course, for many people the actual day of the fiesta is spent recovering from the night before. Fiestas are fun and add to the rich fabric and pattern of life in Spain, as well as creating a pause from the usual frenetic pace of life. After all, in Spain and the Canary Islands, life is for living.

There has been a special fiesta for the whole island of Gran Canaria this week, but it is particularly special for the residents of a pretty town in the north of the island called Teror (not to be confused with terror!). The Virgin of the Pine is the patron saint of Gran Canaria and this fiesta is based upon the story of the Virgin Mary, who made an appearance many years ago.

It was on 8 September 1492 that an image of the Virgin Mary is said to have appeared in a pine tree to Juan Frias, who was the first Bishop of Gran Canaria. Later, a large church was built near to where this pine tree grew, and it is still there today. The original pine tree died a long time ago, but there are more pine trees in the town near to the church.

The Lady of the Pine, or Nuestra Señora del Pino, is said to possess healing qualities, and in true Catholic fund-raising tradition, it is possible to buy wax models of every part of the human body that can be offered for healing.

Visitors to the church will find a beautiful statue of the Virgin, which is taken out of the church in a religious procession every year on 8 September. On this day, people from all across the island come to this small town for a very big fiesta celebration.

Religious or not, many visitors discover that when they are facing the statue of the Virgin it has a powerful and moving effect upon them. It is also rather extraordinary, since one side of the face is smiling and the other side is sad.

The statue has many jewels, but in 1975 there was a robbery at the church and some jewels were stolen from the statue and never recovered.

Thousands of pilgrims joined the procession this week, and many arrived for celebrations on the eve of the fiesta. One of the customs are parrandas or groups of people who move between different places singing traditional songs; others join them to make the singing group larger.

This tradition comes from the islands of Cuba and Puerto Rico, where many people from the Canary Islands moved to many years ago for work. They later returned home and brought with them some of these Caribbean islands' cultures and traditions.

This year's parrandas started with traditional music, but then went on to more modern reggaetron. The singing leads to people dancing until they are ready for refreshment in the local bars. These pilgrims often arrive in Teror by car or bus, but many make the journey on foot, and some this year have been seen dancing in the middle of the GC21 road. Sensibly, for the safety of pilgrims, the main road to Teror was closed to traffic for the evening.

It is noticeable that the traditional grip of the Catholic Church upon people in Spain and the Canary Islands is fast diminishing, and it is rare to see many people attending church on Sundays as used to be the case, particularly during the Franco years. Despite this, it is clear that many Canarians maintain a strong spiritual basis in their lives and continue to be moved and inspired by stories of the saints and religious events, which they celebrate with vigour and enthusiasm. Above all, they enjoy a good party!

The Superstitious Expat

Here we go again, another Friday 13th. I really am fed up with reading what all the doom mongers have to say about the likelihood of disaster on this 'unlucky' day. It reminds me of an event a few weeks ago when a weird religious sect that takes the Book of Revelations literally, busily promoted the idea that the world was about to end on 21 September. How disappointed they must have been on 22 September.

I just hope that they gave some serious thought to those unfortunate believers who committed suicide in order to avoid the big event, or those that had blown all their savings a few weeks before, as they couldn't take their savings with them. Such foolish predictions are not only dangerous lies, but very cruel for many decent, trusting people.

What is it about the human psyche that loves the idea of disaster, terror and fear? Don't we have enough real events to terrorise us already? Do we really need any more demons than 'The Trumper', 'Little Rocket Man', Global Warming, Islamic Terrorism and Harvey Weinstein to successfully chill us to the marrow?

We will shortly have another fiesta, nowadays frantically celebrated in Spain, as well as in many parts of the world. This event is, of course, Halloween, which I personally detest. Gone are the days when it involved little more than drawing a few spooky pictures, hollowing out a pumpkin, and making masks with the kids, with a spot of apple bobbing thrown in for good measure.

We now have an event that to many is little more than the celebration of evil, an opportunity to drink excess alcohol, as well as allowing children to terrorise the neighbourhood. A few years ago, the idea of Halloween, as opposed to the highly religiously significant All Saints Day, was hardly recognised, let alone celebrated in Spain and the Canary Islands.

A commercial opportunity for shops to sell more imported rubbish? Yes, most certainly, but is this kind of celebration healthy, let alone desirable? It is a simple case of 'each to their own' I guess, but I'm having none of it.

In Spain and the Canary Islands, you won't find locals drawing their blinds and running away from black cats. It is actually Tuesday the 13th that is considered to be unlucky, since Tuesday is said to be dominated by Ares, the Greek God of War, who gives his name to the Spanish word for Tuesday, which is Martes. The old Spanish proverb proclaims: 'En martes, ni te cases, ni te embarques, ni de tu casa te apartes' – or in English – "On Tuesday, don't get married, embark on a journey, or move away."

There are also a few more Spanish superstitions that the cautious expats should be aware of, including putting a hat on a bed that will bring bad luck. This superstition is believed to have come from a time when people believed that evil spirits lived in people's hair, which could be transferred from the hair to the hat and then to the bed, leaving unfortunate souls open to ghost attacks during the night.

As a cat lover, one superstition that I am not too keen on in Spain is that cats have only seven and not nine lives as in the UK. Sadly, cats in Spain and the Canary Islands have to be much more careful, since they are two lives short.

I now know never to give a knife as a gift. Spanish tradition states that buying knives or scissors symbolise the cutting of ties and relationships, so if you gift newlyweds with knives, they will break up. That's a pity, since I had planned to give a set of kitchen knives to a lovely couple as a wedding gift. It will just have to be the toaster after all.

Many fans of amateur dramatics in the UK tell their actor friends to 'break a leg', but in Spain it's a bit different. Instead you must wish that person 'mucha mierda', or 'lots of shit'. I shudder to think what the origin of this one is, but I do have a very vivid imagination... If anyone knows the origin of this one, please do let me know.

Have you noticed that many homes in Spain and the Canary Islands have cactus on window sills or placed strategically in their homes? It is believed that spikey green cactus can ward away evil spirits, so a nice prickly cactus might make an appropriate house warming gift. Always be careful when brushing, because you must never sweep the feet of a single woman. If you do, she will never get married and hate you for ever.

Fancy getting your own back on someone? This is easy, just buy them yellow clothes. After all, yellow represents sulphur and the Devil, and it is sure to bring them lots of bad luck. Getting ready for Christmas and the New Year? Don't forget to eat twelve grapes in rapid succession on the stroke of midnight on New Year's Eve. Spanish people reckon that wearing red underwear also helps to bring them good luck, so I must remember to pick up some red undies when next in Marks and Spencer.

By the way, just a tip when eating grapes, please go seedless. I still recall a very unfortunate incident with someone who choked to death on the seventh grape. There really wasn't too much luck involved for him, but maybe he wasn't wearing red underwear.

I'll let readers into a little secret, which may explain a little of my aversion to 'disaster planning' and days that are meant to be unlucky. I was born on Friday 13th at around 13.00. Thanks to my mother's considerable efforts to destroy the myth of 'Unlucky 13', I was taught that Friday 13th is my special day when good things happen.

With one or two notable exceptions, and I won't bore you with the details, this has mostly been the case. Friday 13th is always a good day for me when good things usually happen. I guess it is a state of mind.

I adore black cats, I will happily walk under ladders and never throw spilled salt over my left, or is it right, shoulder. I have no time for superstition and the Book of Revelations. Come on, let's do reality instead. Have a great Halloween!

Britain's Wartime Plan to Invade the Canary Islands

During the current worrying developments in the Spanish autonomous community of Catalonia, many forget that some years ago there was a large and vociferous movement demonstrating for independence for the Canary Islands. Although there are some on the islands that still share this long-term view, much of the debate is currently centred towards peaceful coexistence as a fully functioning autonomous community within Spain.

Some may see Spain's constitution and its wisdom in promoting and allowing autonomous communities to develop and flourish in a manner that reflects the individual and unique culture of its many diverse regions and complicated history as a success.

Spain has come a long way in the years since the repression during the time of the dictator Franco. Despite its problems, Spain has developed rapidly into a modern, welcoming and thriving democracy, currently in the lead with a gross domestic product that beats most other European countries, albeit with a high proportion of its prosperity generated within Catalonia.

For many Spaniards, there is puzzlement over the Catalonia issue; after all, recent studies show that as far as autonomy and self-determination go, Catalonia's rights and freedoms within Spain are far in excess of those allowed in Canada's Quebec and in Scotland as a constituent part of the United Kingdom.

Fighting, the 'grab for land' and the desire for self-determination has always been part of the human psyche. Over the years, history shows us how this destructive aspect of human nature can manifest itself in violence, repression and war. Let us hope that common sense prevails in the current dispute and that talking, negotiation and compromise can reunite during these troubled times.

The British have always loved the Canary Islands, but sometimes for the wrong reasons. A brief wander around Las Palmas will reveal British businessmen honoured in the names of some of its streets, a thriving fruit and vegetable export business originally started by the British, and even a traditional British church for the early businessmen to worship in.

Did you know that the British planned to occupy the Canary Islands, and Gran Canaria in particular, during the Second World War? A current exhibition organised by the Government of Gran Canaria reflects upon the crucial role of the Canary Islands during this period. It is a little-known fact that heads of British military operations were convinced that the Canary Islands were a key factor in the strategic development of the war.

British military planners saw Gran Canaria as a serious alternative should Gibraltar be lost, given the islands' strategic position in the Atlantic. 'Operation Pilgrim' was a military initiative in which the British considered bombing the main infrastructures within the island's capital, Las Palmas, in circumstances when the enemy took Gibraltar, which thankfully never happened.

Moving on to present times, many feel uncomfortable with the name that refers to a popular beach in the south of Gran Canaria, which is currently called 'Playa del Ingles' (The English Beach). For many, it smacks far too much of the British Empire and is a reminder of the negativity and excesses that the Empire stood for. So, how about the locals and the government of the island coming up with a name that truly reflects this beautiful Canarian beach?

Forget Turkey, Eat Tapas!

I remember once being told by an American professor, "History is never taught in American schools". I was puzzled by the comment, since I have always believed that it is history that informs both our present and our future. There is much that we don't understand about the United States; Brits are often puzzled by the phrase "our American cousins", which is a meaningless phrase at the best of times, and particularly when it is over used by UK politicians busily looking for trade deals post Brexit.

Although we speak the same language, cultural differences and values abound, and there are often stark differences, which may be difficult for Europeans to understand. Let me take one example, Thanksgiving, where the Spanish dimension seems to be mostly ignored in favour of a more comfortable version of history.

Very soon people all over the United States will celebrate what they believe to be the first ever Thanksgiving in 1621, gathering together with family and friends and celebrating with traditional turkey and pumpkin pie. I really don't want to spoil this very special day, but it seems that the wrong date and event is being celebrated. It really is time that we had a close look at the facts, as they appear to many historians.

According to American tradition, and not necessarily historical fact, most American school pupils are taught that the first Thanksgiving was celebrated in

1621 by English pilgrims who found refuge in America on the Mayflower.

Archaeologists at Florida's Museum of Natural History contradict this statement, and claim that the first Thanksgiving was actually celebrated in San Augustin, La Florida in 1565, which is 50 years earlier. It was the Spanish explorer Pedro Menéndez de Avilés and a motley collection of 800 soldiers, sailors and assorted settlers, which would have included many conscripts from the Canary Islands who were despatched to help populate the new Spanish colonies.

It was they who celebrated the first Thanksgiving, and not English pilgrims in their wide-brimmed hats as often pictured. It was these new arrivals from Spain who celebrated the first Thanksgiving, which began with a special thanksgiving mass, before enjoying a shared feast with local Native Americans.

Forget traditional turkey and pumpkin pie, because that first Thanksgiving feast included salted pork and typical Spanish food, such as chickpeas and olives, washed down with red wine. It was unlikely that there would be any cranberries, although it is thought that typical Caribbean foods would have been enjoyed, which Menéndez would have thoughtfully collected during his visit to Puerto Rico, as well as a probable stopover in the Canary Islands, before arriving in La Florida.

According to historians, it is thought that the local Timucuan people would also have joined in with the celebrations, adding fresh fish, berries, beans and corn to the feast. The bank of the Matanzas River was the site of the first Spanish colony in the United States, which is where the first Thanksgiving feast took place.

So, why is it that this essential piece of American history appears to have been forgotten or massaged in a way that ignores the natives? Well, as usual, it is thought to be the fault of the British, because the history of the United States has been heavily Anglicised over the centuries, with America's origins seen primarily as British.

This is not the case, since the first colony in the New World was a melting pot that included cultural contributions and interactions with many groups of people, which was totally unlike any other British colony.

The real history of the first Thanksgiving is particularly important in the current political climate, since the Hispanic population in the United States is growing fast. The importance of the Spanish colony in La Florida to American history is rarely taught in schools, let alone understood by the wider population.

The current community of St Augustine founded by Menédez de Avilés on September 8th 1565 has the honour to be the oldest European settlement that has been continually occupied in the country, which in 2015 celebrated its 450th anniversary.

I wish "our American cousins" a happy and peaceful thanksgiving, but urge them to revisit those history books and museum records; forgo turkey and pumpkin pie and instead enjoy tapas and a few glasses of fine Rioja instead. Salud!

Island Culture

The
Canary
Islander

Cuba, Castro and the Canary Islanders

The death of Cuba's former President and Prime Minister, Fidel Castro, has provoked much attention in the media this week. Reaction has covered the entire spectrum of emotion ranging from detestation of a man seen as a tyrant and persecutor of his people, to elaborate praise heaped upon a man seen as saving Cuba from potential ravages and exploitation by the United States.

Whatever the truth, which as always depends upon which side of the political spectrum one is standing, most will agree that Fidel Castro was a controversial and divisive world figure, and someone that could not be ignored. As far as the Canary Islands are concerned, the story of Fidel Castro and his link to these islands has fascinated me for some time.

During the Seventeenth Century, overpopulation of the Canary Islands motivated Spain to 'export' Canarian families to its American colonies in a 'tribute of blood'.

Five Canarian families were sent to a colony in Cuba for every ton of cargo sent, but the numbers of Canarian families emigrating were often much higher. Unemployment in the Canary Islands continued until the Nineteenth Century, when more islanders migrated to Cuba to find work, to avoid starvation and to avoid Spanish military service.

The Twentieth Century was a time when Spain was in the midst of a civil war and firmly in the grip of its dictator, General Franco.

History has been harsh for Canary Islanders who have had to cope with drought, attacks by pirates, locusts, harsh taxes, epidemics and even volcanic eruptions in 1730, so migration to Cuba and other destinations in Central and South America must have been appealing, despite the hardship of the voyage and starting a new life on an island that was so far away from home.

Over time, migrant workers from the Canary Islands, known as Isleños, had a strong influence on the language spoken by Cubans. Spanish spoken in the Canary Islands is different to mainland Spain, but is very similar to Cuban Spanish.

The cigar industry in Cuba was mostly owned by Canarian immigrants, and this led to the cigar industry being established in the Canary Islands as well.

The Spanish dialect spoken by Cubans is most closely associated with the current residents of the island of La Palma, and the influence of Cuba is very strong on this small Canary Island.

Canary Islands' residents currently refer to a bus as a 'guagua', but not 'autobus', which is the usual Spanish word for bus, and 'guagua' is also widely used in Cuba, as well as many other uniquely Canarian words that reflect the shared culture and traditions that link these islands with Cuba.

Mojo sauce served with small wrinkly potatoes cooked in salt water is unique to the Canary Islands, and it is unusual to find this dish in tapas bars in Peninsular Spain, but it is widely served in Cuba, as is gofio and ropa vieja, which is served in many restaurants. The Cuban influence and links are still very strong on these islands.

In a small museum in Aguimes in Gran Canaria, there is a wide range of interesting artefacts about life in the Canary Islands over many years. These artefacts include a height measure, as there had been a minimum height for men planning to migrate to Cuba and other Spanish colonies, as well as a personal letter from President Fidel Castro written to the people of the Canary Islands, in which he recognises the contributions made by Canary Islanders or Isleños to the culture and society of Cuba.

To further emphasise the close links between the Canary Islands and Cuba, as well as other former Spanish colonies in Central and South America, which have been established for hundreds of years, the Spanish Government introduced new legislation in recent years that states that residents of Cuba and other former colonies who are descended from Canary Islanders can apply for Spanish citizenship, and return to live in the Canary Islands or Spain, if they wish.

This reparation of legal rights also recognises that many Canarian families were forced to leave their homes under duress.

Many people living in the Canary Islands had moved to Cuba many years ago to find work, so the culture and lifestyle of Cuba and the Canary Islands share many similarities, and a long history.

Despite the many challenges faced by the Cuban people, and some specific groups like gay and lesbian Cubans who have faced persecution over many years, there will be many Canarians who will remember Fidel Castro's positive achievements with respect for a remarkable leader.

Controversy at the Carnival

In the Canary Islands, as well as in many predominantly Catholic countries around the world, we are currently enjoying a period of collective madness, commonly known as Carnival. Until a few years ago when cheap overseas travel and holidays became readily available, few British people had ever experienced or understood what Carnival was really about; it is certainly not just about amazingly gorgeous dresses, high heels and skimpily dressed girls and guys.

Carnival is part of the Christian, and mostly Catholic, festival season that takes place just before the period known as Lent. It is a period of excess and celebration involving parades, parties, as well as elements of the circus added for good measure. Masks and costumes are worn, together with an excessive consumption of alcohol and food.

Food fights, mockery of authority, satire and exaggeration are the order of the day. Abusive language, exaggerated features, such as mouths, bellies, noses and penises are all part of the fun, with gleeful depictions of death and disease being part of a time when the world is viewed through a different lens with the reversal of what passes for everyday normality.

It is in this context that various Carnival parades are currently taking place in towns and cities all across Spain and the Canary Islands. In Las Palmas de Gran Canaria, for instance, this three-week binge that culminates in a parade that is billed as 'Second only to Rio', vulgarity and tackiness are at their peak.

In Germany too, there were raised eyebrows with one impressive float sporting a huge and colourful effigy of the UK's Brexit Prime Minister, Theresa May, with a loaded pistol marked 'Brexit' pointing into her mouth, no doubt ready to blow her brains out.

Another popular float featured the ever-controversial US President Trump sexually violating the robed and tearful figure 'Libertas', a Roman goddess (of Statue of Liberty fame), which is not a sight for the easily offended or faint hearted, I might add, although it is surprisingly poignant in its message.

Carnival is not always comfortable, since it challenges authority and established views, as well as mocking the status quo; this was one of the reasons why the dictator, General Franco, wanted to ban it in the Canary Islands during Spain's Civil War.

Closer to home, the winner of the Las Palmas de Gran Canaria Carnival Drag Queen competition was won by an artist with an imaginative interpretation of the Virgin Mary that cleverly morphed into Christ's crucifixion; in so many ways, it was a well-deserved win for a talented artist.

I found myself feeling both very impressed, as well as uncomfortable by the performance, which for me was a step too far. The Bishop of the Canary Islands waded into the controversy, reportedly describing the performance as "frivolous blasphemy", and then unwisely commented that it was the saddest day of his time on the Canary Islands, and even more disturbing than the plane crash at Barajas airport of the flight destined for Gran Canaria that claimed the lives of 154 residents and tourists several years ago.

Such comments are not only cruel coming from a man of the cloth, but also upsetting to many people, not least the relatives and friends of the victims. I sincerely hope that the interpretation of the Bishop's words was down to linguistic errors and not an expression of his true feelings.

If so, many would suggest a period of retreat and reflection for the good Bishop to reconcile his views with the feelings of so many who were hurt and offended by his careless comments, whatever his views about blasphemy, of which he has a point.

So, as Carnival comes to an end for another year, with the burial of that blessed sardine once again, we can only reflect and wonder upon the artistry, energy and imagination that so many performers have displayed during these weeks of excess.

On a more serious note, I hope that we are all wise enough to recognise the anger, criticism and defiance of authority that have entered the Carnival parades this year. After all, over the years, Carnival has always reflected the times that we are in; it is also a time when many true and honest feelings are genuinely expressed.

The Perpetual Knife Sharpener

I always admire people who get off their backsides and do something worthwhile with their lives. People, who have an idea, recognise a niche in the market and attempt to fill it with their own hard work, imagination and effort.

Maybe their initiative will lead to something larger than they initially imagined, or maybe it will remain as a useful, but small business. The important thing is that they had a dream, and they succeeded in realising their dream.

It had been haunting me for several years. The sound of panpipes when I was least expecting it finding its tuneful way through open windows or when I was quietly tending the garden. The problem was that I could not link the sound to anyone or anything.

At first, I thought that maybe a neighbour's child was practicing the flute, or a piccolo. Possibly, it was the early onset of insanity, or one too many, since I could not find anyone else who had actually heard it. Some considerable time later, I heard a similar sound in our neighbouring town, but that turned out to be a delivery of bottled gas. Anyway, it was not exactly the same sound, which I would recognise anywhere.

A few days ago, I finally discovered the source of the sound. It comes from a travelling knife sharpener who uses the sound to warn and attract potential customers of his arrival. I caught him in the act one afternoon when I was pruning a tree.

Our boisterous dog, Bella, suddenly heard the noise in the distance and was determined to rescue me from the creator of this strange sound. I stood in the road expectantly watching as the sound became louder and louder. Eventually, an ancient moped came into sight carrying quite a large elderly man. Sadly, he was not actually playing the panpipes that I had imagined, but the same sound was coming from somewhere at the back of his moped.

I waved the man down, and he eventually came to wobbly stop. I asked him what he was doing and where he had come from. It transpired that he was a knife sharpener who had travelled from Las Palmas to sharpen knives, scissors and all manner of cutting instruments that require his services from time to time.

Do you play the panpipes, I asked? Sadly, he did not. He grinned and pointed to a button on his handlebars. He pressed a greasy, green button and the blissful angelic sounds of panpipes sounded from somewhere near the exhaust of his ancient moped.

Alberto, the knife sharpener, travels all over the island, visiting towns and villages where he thinks people are in need of his services. As I had a pair of secateurs, as well as an ancient yet effective long armed trimmer that were both as blunt as a butter knives, I retrieved them and handed them to him.

I wondered if they were too far gone to be rescued, but he smiled, nodded and started the small generator that was attached to his moped. The generator whirred as he ground, smoothed and manicured the rusty metal on the long-neglected secateurs, whilst I stood back and admired how well the moped had been converted. As well as a small generator, the moped had a grinding wheel and other gadgets added, all powered by the generator, to assist in the process of sharpening and grinding.

Several minutes later the secateurs were completed. They looked shiny and felt as sharp as the day that I had bought them. Alberto then moved on to the long arm trimmer, which I had thought about replacing for some time.

This was a much bigger job, and he skilfully ground, smoothed and sanded before he was satisfied with his work. He asked me for some oil, commenting sadly that a teenager had stolen his can of oil earlier that morning. I handed him a can of 'Three-in-One'.

Alberto nodded, as if approving of my choice, and lathered both tools generously with oil before handing them to me. He grinned a toothy smile as he collected the cash.

I asked for his business card or mobile number just in case I wanted to contact him again, as I have several ancient tools in need of some care and restoration. Alberto had neither, but told me that he would be around again in a month or so. He covers most of the island on his moped with generator at the ready, so I guess it will be some time before we see him again.

The Belted Bus

I wonder what readers think about those magic words 'health and safety'? For me, it is usually an excuse for some 'jobsworth' in a government or local authority office trying to stop me from doing something that I really want to do, with nothing more to offer than a feeble, illogical excuse.

Of course, 'health and safety' is important and is intended to be a good thing, but only when it benefits workers, individuals and the wider community, and not as a pointless control mechanism designed to irritate.

In the UK, Germany and much of Scandinavia, 'health and safety' is taken very seriously and there is usually some consistency to the approach. For instance, if you trip on a paving slab, a complaint to the local authority is usually taken seriously and the issue corrected. It can also provide a convenient opportunity for litigation lawyers to pounce and sue the Town Hall on your behalf.

In Mediterranean countries, such as Spain, France and Italy, the issue is generally taken much less seriously. One could kindly say that maybe a more pragmatic and flexible approach is taken to such matters.

I know from several correspondents who have slipped or tripped on tiled pavements or broken concrete stairs in public places, that the response from the Town Hall is often little more than "You should have been more careful". Maybe they have a point.

It was with this in mind that I was surprised to find seat belts fitted to all the seats on a new bus on the island when I caught the bus to Las Palmas this week. There was an incident on the island a few weeks ago when an ancient bus caught fire; fortunately, no one was hurt, but I think it did lead to questions to be asked of the bus company and several new buses were ordered and added to its ageing fleet.

Fitting seat belts in buses is a sensible idea; after all, these valuable safety additions have been compulsory in cars for many years. When we boarded the bus, a warning light shone at the front of the bus to remind passengers to belt up. I noticed an Italian couple with two young children, and an elderly German couple using the belts, but only a few other passengers complied. Still, the thought was there.

This sudden attention to health and safety contrasts starkly with the bus company's policy of allowing up to thirty people to stand in the aisle of the bus during the fifty-minute motorway journey to Las Palmas.

Whilst I fully understand the necessity for occasional standing on crowded, but short bus journeys in the city, asking passengers to stand for the entire journey on a busy motorway, renowned for regular accidents, is nothing short of highly dangerous, as well as uncomfortable. Personally, I no longer cooperate with this, since I would rather get off the bus and wait for the next one.

So, there we have it, a brand-new bus fitted with seat belts, which few people use, whilst the bus company continues to allow passengers to stand in the aisle of a bus filled to capacity on a fast-moving motorway well known for traffic accidents. Logical? No, but then again, few things are... As for health and safety, I guess it is a step in the right direction.

The Cello Epiphany

I often hear from expats who have trouble integrating into their local communities. For some, life may simply revolve around a bar culture, because it is there that they will meet expats like themselves. Other expats often slip happily into fully taking part in local activities and social events for expats, with many also joining in with local community activities, particularly when confidence with their language skills develops.

This was my experience of expat life in the Costa Blanca, where the range and variety of available activities, as well as the willingness of expats to take part always surprised me. Whoever said that the British are reserved?

Of course, there are expats who live in parts of rural Spain and the Canary Islands, where it is not quite so easy to take part in social activities, and particularly when it is necessary to travel at night, with events often beginning at 9.00 pm, and with very little or no public transport available. This is often where hobbies and interests become important if craving for expat television is to be avoided.

A few weeks ago, I was drawn to a sound from a musical instrument that I have not heard for many years. I recognised the instrument immediately and followed the deep, rich, flowing melody to its source. It was a cello, and lovingly played by a young man in the main street of our small town.

I had never seen the cellist before, but he was clearly a highly proficient musician. I sat on the wall nearby and listened as he skilfully made the cello 'speak' to anyone who would listen. I stayed for some time listening and remembering a time when I played the violin in the school orchestra as a teenager.

I remembered that I too had wanted to play one of the school's two cellos, but as I was not particularly skilful, my request was denied and so I was destined to play second violin during my time at the school. Last year, I resumed playing the violin once again after a gap of many years. As is the case with riding a bicycle, early learned skills are not easily forgotten, but it is just more painful with the passage of time!

Over the subsequent weeks, I thought a lot about the cellist and my experience on that sunny morning in town. I found myself searching for and listening to cello music, and particularly performances by soloists.

Eventually, I made up my mind to learn the cello. It was, after all, another stringed instrument, which I am used to. Admittedly, I would not be tucking this instrument under my chin, but a new challenge is good for all of us, isn't it?

Last week, my new cello arrived from Germany. It is a beautiful and amazing instrument that arrived in an enormous box. I had assumed that it would arrive by courier, and was amazed to find our postman struggling to deliver it in his car.

The car seats were folded down, as there was hardly enough room for the postman, let alone the rest of his post. It took two of us to lift the instrument from his car and into our house.

He admitted that he was delighted to be rid of it! Amazingly, my order took less than a week to travel from Germany, which also included a short spell in customs, which again is unusual over here.

So, there we have it; a chance encounter with an unemployed cellist during a shopping trip to my local town has led to what appears to be a life changing experience. I am busily ploughing through the tutor book and enjoying every minute of it. I should also add that most municipalities in Spain offer instrumental music tuition, usually in groups, and at a reasonable cost. So, if you have ever felt the urge to learn the Spanish guitar, now maybe is the time.

Expats be warned. If anyone sends me an email complaining that they are bored with their new lives as expats, I shall now be recommending very firmly that they take up a musical instrument. It is both mentally and physically challenging and may lead to all sorts of social, as well as musical experiences. As for me, I may well consider taking up the Spanish lute (laúd español) next year.

Mummy's Teeth

The recent decision of the Canary Islands' Government to impose a tax on sugar-based food and drinks purchased in the Canary Islands is a response to serious concerns about the very high obesity levels on the islands, which is the third highest region in the world.

Some have claimed that Canarian obesity levels may be linked to genetic factors and not over consumption of sugary foods and drinks. Recent research evidence adds another interesting dimension to this discussion.

Aboriginal Berber people called Guanches were the first settlers of the Canary Islands, migrating to these islands around 1000 BC. Following the Spanish conquest of these islands, those Guanches that survived starvation during a period that many historians now perceive as genocide were quickly absorbed by their Spanish conquerors.

As many visitors to these islands will become aware once they leave the beaches and tourist centres, elements of the rich Guanche culture still survive. Canarian traditions and customs, such as the whistled language of Silbo, practiced on the island of La Gomera, is one example of this rich and varied heritage.

Many secrets of the Guanche past remain hidden and we can only speculate about the life and times of this ancient people. However, one recent discovery tells us much more about their culture, burial practice, health, physique and dental health.

In 2016, one Guanche mummy and three Egyptian mummies were removed from Spain's National Archaeological Museum in Madrid and taken for a detailed scan that would hopefully yield much more information than previously known.

Although the mummified body of the Guanche showed many similarities with its Egyptian counterparts, the main difference was that the Egyptians removed the brains and internal organs, whilst the Guanches left the organs of their dead intact at the time of mummification.

Remembering that these bodies were preserved more that 2000 years ago, the results are fascinating. Two of the Egyptian mummies were found to be women, one of whom was pregnant. A third mummy was a male who was a doctor to the Pharaoh and priest in the 27th Century BC.

It was the mummified body of the Guanche from Santa Cruz, Tenerife that will be of most interest to many Canarians. This Guanche mummy, who lived between the 11th and 13th Century B.C. and was discovered in a cave in the Herques Valley in Tenerife in 1763, revealed that mummies from the Canary Islands had better dental health than their Egyptian counterparts.

Many high-resolution anatomical images reconstructed the bodies in 3D, revealing necklaces, bracelets, a diadem, sandals and 16 amulets. As well as bones, researchers found fragments of ligaments, tendons, muscles and the heart in the Egyptian mummies, even though they had their internal organs removed, since they believed that was where the essence of being and feelings resided.

The study of the Guanche mummy revealed that mummies from the Canary Islands had far better teeth than their Egyptian counterparts, whose dental health was very poor. This research is further proof that the Guanches lived on a low-sugar diet.

It was much later when the Canary Islands became the site of the first Spanish-owned sugar plantations in the 15th Century that the islands became dependent upon a sugar-based economy. Maybe that is when sugar-based health and obesity problems began…

El Hierro, Sailors and the Virgin

I will shortly be making another visit to one of my favourite Canary Islands, the Island of El Hierro. Despite being the smallest of the islands in physical size, it is an island crammed with natural wonders, such as sea cliffs, lush forests and volcanic features to admire.

Each of the Canary Islands is different, and El Hierro has become particularly special, and famous in environmental circles, due to its imaginative efforts in making the island self-sufficient from oil, relying upon water and wind power, of which it has plenty, to generate the electricity that the island needs.

Electric cars, complete with charging points, and free Wi-Fi across the island are both modern technological factors that add to the special appeal of this island, which is in sharp contrast to the ruggedness and remoteness of an island that appears almost untouched by tourism.

Occasional volcanic eruptions can be a slight disincentive for some tourists, although I suspect that this will change rapidly following the introduction of a 75 per cent travel discount for all residents of the Canary Islands.

Inter-island travel is usually quite expensive, and discounted travel is a wise initiative from the Canary Islands Government, which should assist both communication and tourism.

The Descent of the Virgin of the Kings (Bajada de la Virgen de Los Reyes) is celebrated on the first Saturday of July every four years. The procession carries the statue of the Virgin from its hermitage to the island's capital, Valverde, a journey of around 29 kilometres.

La Bajada is an extraordinary procession, accompanied by dancers dressed in traditional white and red dresses, wearing multi coloured hats, and accompanied by the sounds of many castanets and drums.

The whole island joins in the celebrations, which begins at the Hermitage of the Kings, at the west of the island, followed by lunch at 'The Cross of the Kings', arriving in Valverde during the evening.

Celebrations take place during the entire month of July, with the statue of the Virgin visiting the most important towns and centres on the island, until the first Saturday of August, when it is returned to the hermitage. La Bajada is based upon a fascinating story that has become the focal point of the fiesta.

In 1546, a ship passed along the coast of El Hierro destined for the Americas. However, the ship could not leave the Sea of Calm due to a lack of wind, so the ship was forced to sail in a circle for several days.

Finally, on January 6 the food on board had run out and the sailors were forced to ask the islanders of El Hierro for food. Shepherds willingly gave the sailors the supplies for the harsh journey ahead, and without accepting payment.

In return and in thanksgiving, the sailors gave the shepherds the only item of value that they kept on the ship, which was an image of the Virgin Mary. From this moment onwards, a gentle breeze began to blow in the Sea of Calm and the ship could recommence its journey.

The shepherds carefully guarded the Virgin in honour of the day that the sailors arrived on the island. The carving was placed in a cave where she was venerated and offered gifts. The Virgin became the protector and patroness of the whole island.

It has occurred to me that having a celebration of this kind every four years is a rather good idea, and wonder if a similar pattern should be implemented for many other fiestas that seem to come around rather too quickly for me to catch up?

Imagine Christmas, Easter, Halloween and the entire collection of fiestas taking place every four years; it would give us all much more time to catch our breath, as well as to save up for the big event. However, I guess that the Church and commercial interests, such as shops and manufacturers and children, would not be too keen. Maybe it is not such a good idea after all.

A Cave Holiday

"Top 20 Caves to Rent in the Canary Islands" screams one advertisement, followed by "Hundreds of Cave Homes to Buy in the Canary Islands" shouts another.

Well, I guess it all makes good copy, but is living in a cave just another symptom of 'reverse one-upmanship', and something to brag about to colleagues at work? "Oh, I'm just off to the cave for the weekend."

During the Spanish conquest of the Canary Islands, the native aborigines, the Guanches, were considered to be living at a primitive level by European standards. The Guanches wore animal skins for clothing, made stone tools for hunting and lived in caves. Well, if that's not primitive, what is?

It is strange how with the passage of time, reverting back to cave dwelling is seen as 'cool' (in more ways than one) and is now a highly desirable form of accommodation for some.

A few weeks ago, we visited a friend whom we have known for many years. He bought a group of caves in the Canary Islands before it became fashionable and at a knock down price too. He and his family were not living in exactly slum-like conditions, since our friend's caves were well equipped with all modern conveniences.

There is running water and mains electricity, although many cave dwellers prefer to rely upon their own solar installations, since it gives them a feeling of self-sufficiency. Beautifully designed bedrooms, fitted kitchen, sauna and games room would put most homes to shame, with the added benefits of fast Internet connection and cable television. Our friend's home included a patio and delightful, well-stocked garden crammed full with unusual and native plants.

There are many such cave homes throughout the Canary Islands, with the most villages made up of cave homes located in Gran Canaria, where the excavation of cave homes into the mountain side remains a feature of the natural landscape.

One of the most appealing features of cave homes is that it is unlikely that air-conditioning in summer and heating in winter are needed, since they remain at a steady temperature throughout the year. How's that for energy efficiency?

Visitors to the Aguimes municipality in Gran Canaria will also find some of the best-preserved cave dwellings on the island in the Guayadeque ravine. There are several cave restaurants and even a cave church that is open to visitors, which may help visitors to appreciate the sense of coolness and atmosphere of cave dwellings.

If we now hop over to another of the Canary Islands, Lanzarote, visitors will discover a cave home in the middle of a remote lava field. This was the dream home of the renowned artist, César Manrique who utilised the simple idea of living in five volcanic chambers.

This is not an ordinary home, but one lovingly created by a man who had the vision to develop Lanzarote's unique volcanic landscape into an ecologically friendly dwelling. It is thanks to Manrique that regulations were brought into being to restrict tourism development on the island with any structure taller than a palm tree forbidden.

Homes are not the only use for caves in Lanzarote, with a cafe built into a rock on the island's north coast and a theatre, swimming pool and nightclub built into another cave complex, which was hugely admired by Manrique as the world's most beautiful cave adaption - praise indeed.

Of course, as time goes on, modern adaptions of original cave homes distort our vision of the lives and times of these early people. As a reminder, visitors to Gran Canaria may wish to visit one of the most important archaeological sites in the Canary Islands, the Cueva Pintada (the Painted Cave), which interprets life at the time of the Guanches.

The original purpose of the cave is unknown, but it is decorated with red, black and white painted geometrical shapes and may have been used as a dwelling, a scared place or for funeral rites. This spectacular site is well worth a visit.

So, before you rush off to book your modern cave home experience with Airbnb, and yes, I have no doubt that a version of a cave home will be available on there too, do give some thought to these ancient people and the lives that the Guanches lived before the invasion by their Spanish conquerors and the genocide that was to follow. Personally, I'd rather book a nice hotel.

The Story of Nelson, a Lost Arm and the Smelly Cheese

Many will have read stories and been taught about one of the UK's national heroes, Horatio Nelson; that brave son of Norfolk who taught the Spanish a thing or two during his famous battles, his "mesmerising personality", complicated love scandal and heroic death.

The stories surrounding Nelson are, of course, based upon the British point of view. Are they true? How about looking at Nelson from the Spanish and Canarian perspective?

About 220 years ago, Admiral Nelson of the British Royal Navy decided to attack Santa Cruz in Tenerife to help himself to some gold and silver collected by Spanish galleons from the Americas, but was humiliatingly and satisfyingly defeated by the local residents. I guess this part wasn't stressed too strongly during school history lessons, was it?

The residents of Santa Cruz de Tenerife have long memories of their history and proudly re-enact an historical event each year on 25 July that reminds everyone of the Battle of Santa Cruz in 1797. This re-enactment of this battle has taken place for many years in a variety of formats. Why was this battle so important to the people of Tenerife?

In 1797 the British Royal Navy decided to attack the port of Cadiz in Southern Spain, but Spanish warships drove the British away. By chance, the British Navy heard that Spanish treasure convoys from America arrived regularly at Santa Cruz in Tenerife, and sent a flotilla of ships under the command of the recently promoted Admiral Nelson.

This attack force had 4000 men, nine ships and 400 guns, but the military on Tenerife led by Lieutenant General Gutierrez only had 91 guns and a mixture of 1700 militia and sailors. This looked to be an overwhelming attack force with insufficient military to defend the port of Santa Cruz.

Things did not work out as planned for Nelson, as the Tenerife commander was more experienced and particularly clever in managing his soldiers. Several British ships were sunk and many sailors were killed in this failed attack.

This was also the battle when Admiral Nelson was shot in his right arm, and he had to be taken back to his ship where the ship surgeon amputated most of this arm with the help of some opium to lessen the pain in the middle of the battle.

Many British militias became trapped on the shores of Tenerife with no escape possible. Although 30 Tenerife residents were killed and 40 were injured; 250 British militia were killed and 128 were wounded.

The British asked for a truce and agreed to withdraw with an undertaking to do no further damage to the town or to make any more attacks on Tenerife or the Canary Islands. This was agreed by Lieutenant

General Gutierrez, who also allowed the British to leave with their arms, but perhaps not Nelson.

However, Admiral Nelson had lost so many ships that he did not have capacity to take all his militia back home, so the Tenerife General lent Nelson two Spanish schooners. This was a huge embarrassment for the British Navy and a resounding success for the militia of Tenerife in protecting their island. I doubt that much of this story has found its way into the National Curriculum syllabus, as it really does not show the British in a particularly good light.

There are also some interesting facts that are linked to the Battle of Santa Cruz, such as what happened to Nelson's right arm after it was amputated? It was thought that the arm was thrown overboard after the on-board operation, as was usual during this period, but it seems that some keen-eyed Tenerife resident found this floating in the sea or washed ashore, and eventually Nelson's arm ended up interred within the altar of the Cathedral of Las Palmas de Gran Canaria.

This story has been challenged, but it has not been denied either! Also, the honourable withdrawal and truce led to a courteous exchange of letters between Nelson and Gutierrez. Later, Nelson sent a large cheese to Gutierrez as a token of his gratitude, which was never eaten and is still on display at the Spanish Army Museum in Toledo in Peninsular Spain. Maybe the good General did not trust the British to send a cheese that wasn't poisoned?

No doubt the British will hope that people will forget the Battle of Santa Cruz de Tenerife in 1797 and the humiliating defeat that the brave people of Tenerife achieved over the British Navy. However, the residents of Santa Cruz in Tenerife are determined never to forget this momentous day in their history. Many wear faithful reproductions of uniforms and weapons of this historical period in all its detail of the battle in July.

Many might think that Tenerife residents would hate Admiral Nelson as he had planned to rob them and destroy their homes, but actually he became admired as he stuck to his word and the British Navy never returned to attack the Canary Islands. Indeed, there is one street in Santa Cruz that is named 'Avenida Horacio Nelson', which says a great deal about the island's capacity for forgiveness, or is it amusement?

Anyway, the Canary Islands still have Nelson's arm in their possession, or maybe not, but it definitely has a smelly cheese as a result of this battle from long ago.

The Stinky Tree

It is often fascinating to discover some of the remedies and answers to problems that can be found by looking at the past. If we look carefully, we often find answers to many present-day problems, and how our ancestors dealt with the inconveniences of life. I discovered this recently when looking at a tree on the small island of El Hierro.

A visit to the enchanting island of El Hierro is not complete without a visit to see the Stinkwood or Smelly tree (Ocotea foetus), which is native to the island. The tree is evergreen, a member of the laurel family, and is threatened due to the loss of habitat in the areas where it thrives and, I suspect, its pungent aroma.

Yes, it can be smelly, hence the name, because the tree is rich in essentials oils. These oils give off an unpleasant odour to the wood when cut, but don't let this part of the story put you off. After all, stinky or not, this tree does have an interesting story to tell...

The Stinkwood tree was sacred to the ancient inhabitants of the small Canary Island of El Hierro, the Bimbaches, who called it the Garoe. Legend states that the Garoe assured the life of the Bimbaches, because it provided them with sufficient water to ensure their survival. Remember, this was not a time when the locals could pop into the local shop and buy a large bottle.

The Canary Islands are visited by the trade winds and, since water was so scarce, the little water that was available to these ancient islanders were from the clouds that condensed on the branches of the tree. It is said that water that dripped from this tree was led to a hole from which the Bimbaches took their water supply.

The original Garoe tree was destroyed by a storm on the island, but in 1957 a replacement tree was planted in the same location as the original tree. Legend or not, the same principles as deployed by these ancient people are still just as relevant to fulfilling islanders need for water today.

Let us now move to another Canary Island, Fuerteventura, where similar principles for catching water are still used. The Fuerteventura Government has been collecting mist for the last year or two, and this new technology has already collected over 33,000 litres of water.

Mist collectors use humidity from the trade winds that blow across Fuerteventura, and extract water from mist and fog to create a sustainable water supply. Meters fitted to the mist collectors show around 6,500 litres of water are collected each month during the trade winds season.

So, how is this done in Fuerteventura without the assistance of the Garoe tree? This simple technology uses mesh placed on vertical structures in high mountain areas that intercept mist and humidity that blows across them, and water droplets fall into storage tanks.

These mist collectors use water from sea mist or clouds to support the reforestation of endemic or specific species of plants and trees, which will help plant habitats to recover by providing moisture for the soil and improve the quality of the environment and landscape.

It is both a humbling and fascinating thought that technology and processes used by the ancient people in the Canary Islands are being brought back into use today in an effort to rectify damage caused to the environment over many centuries.

The Korean Factor

It was a pleasant surprise this week to read that the Mayor of Las Palmas de Gran Canaria is visiting South Korea to exchange ideas and experiences about policies on public transport, and a range of other issues. It makes a pleasant change to read positive news about South Korea, rather than depressing and unpleasant rhetoric, sabre rattling and threats between their neighbour, North Korea, and the United States.

Transport has been a major challenge to authorities in Seoul for the last 40 years, because of the rapid increase in its population. Bus and subway systems have required massive investment and improvements, which are some of the issues also being faced in Las Palmas.

The sharing of information, including the new Metro Guagua transport system in La Palmas, could also be of significant help to Seoul. Representatives from Seoul have been invited to visit Las Palmas when the Metro Guagua is in operation.

The possibility of Canarian and South Korean Municipalities working together on a number of strategic projects has also been discussed, as well as investment from South Korea for projects in Gran Canaria. Cooperation and sharing of ideas between countries should always be welcomed.

Links between South Korea and the Canary Islands are not accidental. Many residents and tourists are simply unaware that there is a significant Korean population living in the Canary Islands, and particularly in Gran Canaria.

This has developed since the collapse of the Korean whaling industry that took place off the Canary Islands in the 1960s and 1970s. Hundreds of Korean workers and their families became stranded on the island, which quickly became their home. In the 1970s, statistics show that there were around 7000 Koreans living in Las Palmas, which became a significant proportion of the total population.

As delighted as I am that the whaling industry has ended off the Canary Islands, the Korean community has thrived and become interwoven with the multi-cultural, multinational and religious mix that Gran Canaria has represented so successfully for many years.

Korean families have also maintained their strong religious and cultural identity. I recall being invited and welcomed to a service held at the spectacular Full Gospel Korean Church in Las Palmas several years ago, where the service was simultaneously broadcast in several languages. Rarely have I witnessed such enthusiasm and fervour within a church.

As well as representation through the Korean Consulate in Las Palmas, which is one of several in Spain, many Koreans run successful businesses on the island. Taking into account the close links that the island has had with Korea over the years, and the significant positive contribution that Koreans have upon both the city of Las Palmas, as well as Gran Canaria, it is entirely appropriate that these links both support and extend the current transportation projects for the benefit of both communities.

I'm Just Having a Tertulia

One of my favourite cafe bars is called 'La Tertulia'. It is not a particularly grand establishment and is completely unlike any of those overpriced and often pretentious coffee shops that are springing up in city centres all over the UK. Our 'Tertulia' is a friendly and welcoming safe space where good coffee and delicious snacks are served at a fair price. Customers are welcome to stay for as long as they wish; it is an oasis of calm in a busy world.

Usually, the Tertulia is an oasis of calm, but on occasions opinions become heated, voices are raised to such a disturbing decibel level that only the Spanish and Canarians are able to achieve. Generally, though, discussions are well mannered and good natured.

The Spanish language fascinates me, and like so many expats I have been guilty of many delicious misinterpretations of Spanish words within an English context. Before I managed to become more fluent with my Spanish, I mistakenly thought that 'tertulia' simply meant a type of tortilla.

Later, for some unknown reason, our special cafe bar became known as 'The Turtle Bar'. Later, of course, when I bothered to consult my Spanish-English dictionary, I realised that 'tertulia' meant something completely different, but entirely appropriate and special.

The definition of 'La Tertulia' is basically that of a social gathering, often with an artistic or literary dimension, which is popular in Latin America and Spain. The word often refers to an informal group of like-minded people talking about local and national news, and politics.

Historically, a typical tertulia was a regularly scheduled meeting in a public place, such as a bar, although sometimes such events were held in someone's living room. Those participating were known as contertulios, and in the creative context, often used the opportunity to share poetry, short stories, songs and art.

The Spanish and Canarians love to talk, preferably loudly, and delight in the company of others, and particularly with like-minded people. Indeed, some of the programmes on Spanish television may contain elements of 'La Tertulia' with invited guests taking part in a heated discussion.

Another explanation that makes quite a lot of sense is that, traditionally, many Spanish men did not like to clear the table or do the washing up after a meal. Cleverly, they came up with the idea that the local bar would serve a better coffee than that produced at home. Sadly, many Spanish women let their partners get away with it, which essentially gave free reign to the idea of 'La Tertulia'.

'La Tertulia' is said to have really taken off in the Sixteenth Century, because King Phillip II of Spain became very interested in the ancient world and its cultures. As a result of his growing interest, he employed experts to compose poetry intended to accompany the artwork displayed in various palaces.

Academics and courtiers would meet together to discuss their work with the King, which resulted in 'La Tertulia' developing as a term for learned discussion between like-minded individuals.

Back to our coffee shop in the Canary Islands; let us not get too high minded and academic about tertulias, since this is not the tertulia that I recognise. Basically, most folk call into our tertulia for just a good gossip over delicious coffee.

Staying Legal

Another Number to Remember

Our lives are punctuated, as well as defined, by numbers. How many of us can remember them all? We have National Insurance numbers, car registration numbers, mobile phone numbers, PIN numbers and all the rest. For expats in Spain, another number is required that is probably the most important one of them all, the NIE.

Expats arriving in Spain and the Canary Islands who intend to remain for a period of time, quickly realise that they need to register with the local Town Hall and police station before they can achieve anything worthwhile; they need an NIE number.

These letters stand for 'Numero de Identificacion de Extranjero', which means 'foreigners identification number'. It is a series of numbers currently beginning with the letter 'X' and ends with another letter.

When we moved to Spain, achieving the exulted status of someone with an NIE was not easy. I recall queuing for several days outside an office in Alicante, only to be turned away when the magic quota for the day, of around 100 NIEs, had been issued.

We would then take our place very early the following morning, complete with picnic chairs, a bottle of water and a pack of sandwiches, for the same process to be repeated. It the end, we became so angry that we made a deal with a local car salesman from whom we had planned to purchase a car once we had obtained the NIE.

We told him that we would only purchase a car from him if he obtained an NIE number for us. Surprisingly, we both had our NIE within 24 hours of the deal being made.

So why is this number so important? When expats want to open a bank account they will need their NIE number, as well as for buying a car, taking out a contract for electricity and water, taking out insurance, asking for a mobile phone contract or SIM card, buying or renting a property, applying for a mortgage and selling a property.

The NIE number is also needed when living and working in Spain, as this is used for completing tax forms, opening a new business, and applying to register as self-employed. In short, you can do very little in Spain legally without it.

Foreigners who wish to become resident in Spain must provide proof that they have private health insurance, or proof of paying into Spain's own insurance scheme for expats that gives access to the Spanish National Health Service.

In addition, foreigners must be able to prove that they have enough funds to support themselves and their family, or prove that they have a contract of employment, or intend to register as self-employed.

Many expats moving to Spain use an English-speaking lawyer to help them to apply for an NIE number if they do not speak Spanish fluently.

Nowadays, I usually suggest that newly arrived expats employ a 'Gestor' or an 'Asesor' who can do some of the nifty footwork needed for some of the bureaucratic high jumps that are necessary when moving to Spain. An NIE is usually produced swiftly and without complication, assuming of course that the correct paperwork is available to allow this to happen.

Expats can, of course, do this for themselves, but they need to be able to speak good Spanish in order to understand and complete the process. An NIE number can be applied for at any foreigners' office and some police stations, which are listed on the Direccion General de la Policia website.

It is important to carefully check exactly what documents are needed, as these vary from region to region, between offices, as well as between the members of staff dealing with the application!

It is necessary to complete a form requesting an NIE, the 'Solicitud de Numero de Identidad de Extranjero y Certificados', known as EX15, which should be presented with a passport size photo of the applicant and a photocopy of the passport, but the original passport always needs to be shown as well.

Usually a date is given when the NIE can be collected from the office, and applicants are also given a form to take to a bank to pay the current fee for completion. The proof of payment given by the bank is then taken to the foreigners' office where the precious NIE certificate can be collected.

Some regions insist that the applicant visits the foreigners' office at least for collection. Application times vary across the Spanish regions, but these offices should be able to give an approximate timescale.

Many expats may wish to undertake tasks such as this for themselves, since it is all part of the expat experience and gives a fascinating insight into life in bureaucratic Spain. It can also be an amusing experience, if they participate in the right frame of mind and do not exhibit anger or frustration at the inevitable delays or requests for yet another document.

My last piece of essential advice is to stress the importance of always taking along a picnic chair, bottle of water and a pack of sandwiches – just in case!

Tricked by the Insurance Company

I occasionally receive emails from expats who have fallen foul of insurance companies in their adopted countries. The problem is usually a lack of understanding of the cultural differences in terms and conditions, as well as language issues. Two readers, Debbie and John, raised an issue with me this week about property insurance.

The couple bought an apartment in the Costa Blanca about ten years ago, with the help of a mortgage from a Spanish bank. At the time of the purchase, the bank also insisted that they take out the bank's property and contents insurance, which the couple did not think unreasonable at the time.

Over the years, the couple paid their annual premium, but were irritated that the premium was always drawn from their bank account <u>before</u> they received their renewal notice. Again, this issue seems to be a regular pattern with insurance and utility companies in Spain, and is a blatant attempt to prevent customers from switching to another company at the time of renewal.

On two occasions over the years, the couple had to make small claims for damage to their home, and had become annoyed and disillusioned with the insurance company for their lack of courtesy and efficiency in dealing with their problems.

Their many phone calls to the company were usually neither answered nor returned, which led the couple to wonder what would happen if they had a really serious problem that required their assistance.

The final straw came in November 2016, when Debbie called the company to ask what their likely premiums would be from January 2017, since the premiums had increased substantially the previous year. The poor response from the company was enough to convince Debbie that they should change insurance companies at the end of the year.

The couple decided to insure their property with the same company that insured their car; not only would they receive a substantial discount on premiums, but they trusted the company having had a claim several years earlier, which had been well handled. As a bonus, the company had English speaking staff and the insurance policies were provided both in English and Spanish.

John went to the bank and cancelled the direct debit to the insurance company. He also wrote a letter to the company, explaining that they were dissatisfied and would not be renewing their policy in January. In addition, he sent a copy of the letter by fax to the head office of the company, knowing how much Spanish companies still value the humble fax machine.

Content in the knowledge that their home was now insured with a company that they could trust, Debbie and John went back to the UK for a few weeks. On their return, they were surprised to see a letter from the previous company confirming renewal of the old policy. John telephoned the company and after several attempts managed to speak to someone who told them that they couldn't cancel the policy, as they had not received a cancellation letter within the one month period prior to expiry; they were expected to pay the premium for another full year.

Over the next few weeks, there was a heated exchange of letters and phone calls between the couple and the insurance company demanding the premium. Despite having sent both a letter and fax, John had no receipts to prove that these had been sent. The situation turned into one of blame with the company denying receipt of the letter of cancellation, whilst John and Debbie argued that they had complied fully with the company's terms and conditions.

Speaking to several banking and insurance contacts on Debbie and John's behalf, it seems that their experience is not unusual and appears to be usual practice in Spain, with expats being particularly vulnerable to coercion. Once a policy is cancelled, many insurance companies will continue to demand unpaid premiums, make threats by telephone and letter as well as threatening court action for a period of time. In some cases, they take the premium from the bank without the customer's permission. The advice is clear:

Ensure that you give at least 30 days' notice of cancellation to the insurance company, in Spanish.

Send the letter 'certificado', ensuring that you retain the Correos receipt and track safe receipt of the letter, if possible.

Send a copy of the letter by fax, and retain the 'send and receipt' slip provided by the machine.

If the company denies receiving correct cancellation of the policy, send them copies of the receipts (again, send signed for), and ignore further communications from them. In most cases, the threats will cease after a few weeks, and in only rare cases is it worth the insurance company's trouble and expense in taking legal action against the policyholder.

If the insurance company takes the money from a bank account without permission, insist upon a refund of the premium from the bank within 45 days of the transaction taking place.

Sadly, the ombudsman and complaints systems for banking and insurance are not as well advanced as in the UK, which is also a problem for those expats who have little understanding of the language. The insurance companies know this and many are only too willing to take advantage to boost profits.

Expat property owners with mortgages from Spanish banks should be aware that they are not obliged to accept a policy suggested by the bank, who also provides the mortgage. Customers are at liberty to shop around and find the best deal with a company with a proven track record of good claims support and customer service. The bank may insist upon a copy of the new policy, together with an entry in the policy document confirming that the bank has an interest in the property, together with the mortgage account number, which is a reasonable request.

Despite this issue, there are some good insurance companies in Spain, who provide a high-level of customer service and support when it is most needed. Some companies also offer excellent support in English too, which is helpful at times of crisis. It is a question of shopping around, but not only for price. It is also important to speak to other expats who have had experience of claiming from a company; after all it is help when you need it urgently that is most important.

More Trickery by the Insurance Company

Several weeks ago, I wrote an article about some of the insurance companies in Spain pressuring, and using what many would see as underhand methods, to coerce expats into renewing their buildings insurance policies, even though they have been cancelled.

I have been surprised by the number of emails that I have received about this issue. A far larger group of expats have felt intimidated by insurance companies, both in Spain as well as other European countries, than I initially imagined.

In some cases, policyholders failed to understand, through both language and cultural factors, that most Spanish insurance companies require at least one month's notice of intention to terminate an insurance policy.

Despite doing this, I have heard from many expats who have written to cancel, telephoned, emailed and sent faxes, only to find that their bank account has been debited for the amount of the renewal premium, and that their instructions to cancel the policy have been ignored.

Peter in the Costa Blanca emailed me to say that as well as writing and faxing his insurance company one month before the policy was due to expire, the insurance company took the money from his bank account. Peter contacted the bank and received a refund, but the insurance company is still pestering him for a full one year of premiums, which he continues to refuse to pay.

Peter makes the comment that "I'm sure it is only expats who are targeted in this way. From what I hear from Spanish friends, they would simply ignore it."

It is not always this easy though, as Sarah and George from Tenerife will testify. This elderly couple have been plagued with endless telephone calls each morning and most evenings for the last two months. The calls are in "machine gun Spanish", and the couple find it difficult to understand what is being said, other than the demand that they pay 420 euros for a policy that they no longer want. The couple are becoming so anxious about the calls that they are about to change their telephone number.

Another expat, Crystal, from Murcia, told me about her insurance company who demanded her bank details, despite preferring to pay cash at the local office. As well as later taking money from her bank account without prior notification, the company refused to cancel the policy even though Crystal had taken out a new policy with another company.

The company's response was that in the case of a claim, Crystal could choose which company to claim from! Crystal was the only expat that I have heard from who took the time and trouble to contact the Insurance Ombudsman who is supposed to help to resolve disputes between insurance companies and clients. Sadly, the Ombudsman didn't reply to Crystal's complaint.

I was even more concerned to receive an email from Godfrey, another reader in the Costa Blanca, who told me that he was so afraid of the letters that he had received, he paid the company even though he didn't need the policy. "I have always tried to do the right thing in Spain. I do my best to obey the law and to fit in. I was worried that they might take me to court and, because of Brexit, I would lose my right to live in Spain".

In the original article, I had intended to include a list of 'Saints and Sinners' on the 'Expat Survival' website, based on recommendations and complaints from expats. I had not realised that some of the companies that I thought would be on the 'Saints' list have actually treated expats very badly. Indeed, it seems that most Spanish insurance companies are behaving badly, and in these circumstances, it is very hard to produce a 'Saints' list with any confidence.

As the previous article explains, situations where companies remove money from your bank account are easy to rectify. Simply go to your bank and ask them to revoke the transaction. You have 45 days to do this and it is a simple procedure. The issue is more complicated when the insurance company claims not to have received your instructions to cancel.

Although it is a question of their word against yours, lack of evidence in the form of a receipt from the post office, confirmation of fax etc. makes it highly likely that the insurance company will continue to harass their client through letters and phone calls until the unfortunate expat pays up. Many expats simply pay up because of fear. In most cases, my best advice is to ignore the phone calls and letters, and it will eventually go away.

What Are the British Well Known For?

The British used to be well known across the world for Shakespeare, Princess Diana and cricket. We like to be known for our infamous 'stiff upper lips', sense of fair play, tolerance and justice. Many, mostly older people, still like to revel in the days of Empire and the 'enlightenment' that it brought to the world, whilst conveniently forgetting the evils of slavery, repression and imposition of alien values upon people across the world.

No doubt, we all have an image of what Britain and its people stand for, although younger members of society are developing rapidly different views, which is very welcome in a fast moving, modern world.

In the years that I have been living as an expat in Spain and the Canary Islands, I have come to a view, which many will regard as unreasonable and non-liberal, that British citizens should first pass an intelligence test and secondly a test in basic good manners before they are granted a British passport.

Many expats like myself, and the majority of British holidaymakers, are appalled by the attitudes and behaviour of a small minority of British holidaymakers.

Over the years, we have become familiar with the chancers who claim to have had valuable items 'stolen' on holiday and attempt to claim the proceeds from their insurance company. It doesn't take a genius to work out that a family heading for one of the cheapest holidays in Benidorm is unlikely to own a top-quality Rolex watch, the latest iPhone, diamond bracelet and expensive camera for each member of the family.

Fortunately, the Spanish police are now much more rigorous in investigating such claims, and offenders are likely to be arrested and prosecuted for fraud. In addition, insurance companies are now much wiser to such scams, sharing databases of claims and identifying potential fraud. Despite this, we still regularly hear of such claims, although most are refused and the perpetrators prosecuted for fraud.

As many will have read in recent weeks, the latest British scam, and I stress that so far it is only the British who are involved, is false claims for food poisoning against hotels in Spain and the Canary Islands, even though the holidaymakers have not been genuinely ill.

There are 'legal companies' in the UK, who are now presumably at a loose end following the completion of banking PPI compensation claims, and are now encouraging holidaymakers to claim for food poisoning. Many claimants have received large sums of compensation from innocent Spanish hotels, because the hotels cannot afford the high costs of challenging such claims in the British courts, and have simply paid up without a challenge.

These 'legal companies' have been offering 'no win, no fee' arrangements to hundreds of British holidaymakers, costing Spanish hotels around 60 million euros, which is a situation that clearly cannot continue. Spanish hoteliers and the Spanish

Government are now fighting back and all future claims will have to be heard in Spanish courts.

Some hotels are now refusing to accept British guests, and those that are accepted are being carefully monitored, with the introduction of signed disclaimers, and in 'all inclusive' hotels, the quantity of food and drinks consumed during the supposed period of illness is being recorded. In addition, ringleaders will be identified and prosecuted.

It was good to read this week that two British people were arrested by the Guardia Civil in Mallorca for trying to persuade tourists to make fraudulent claims whilst staying in the resort of Alcudia. The couple were acting for a so-called legal company in the UK that is sending representatives to Spanish resorts to drum up more business, as they are clearly making massive profits. The main regions affected by these fraudulent claims are the Canary Islands, Costa Blanca, Benidorm, Mallorca and the Costa del Sol.

Probably, my suggestion for a test of intelligence and basic good manners before being granted a British passport should be regarded as 'tongue in cheek', but it is worrying that a small minority of our fellow citizens are behaving in a manner that eventually has a negative impact upon all.

I suspect that if the question is currently asked about what the British are known for, it will no longer be Shakespeare, Princess Diana and cricket.

Finding a Home

The
Canary
Islander

Getting Tough on Builders

Since the World economic recession in 2008, and many would say long before that, builders and developers have been accused of holding onto land that has been agreed for development purposes in the hope that eventually it will increase in value. At that time, and only when the price of land and property shows a significant mark up, will building work be completed.

As we have seen in the Canary Islands, Spain, as well as in the United Kingdom, the result of this approach has been a shortage of affordable housing due to building projects being put on hold or abandoned.

Many young families in the Canary Islands still live with their parents with little hope of ever being able to afford to rent or buy a home of their own. Despite promises from governments, it is likely that it will be many years before promises can be fulfilled, if ever.

As far as repairs to infrastructure is concerned, one Spanish municipality has had enough and is going to take drastic action against such lethargy in the name of profit, which many would say is long overdue. The plan is to clamp down on developers that have not completed work that had been agreed.

The Department of Planning will seize around 500,000 euros worth of bonds, which builders and promoters are obliged to lodge with the municipality at the planning stage, for agreed road repairs, pavements and public areas. These bonds are required at the initial stage of granting all building licences for the main purpose of ensuring that work is completed.

This sum is linked to around 60 permits that date back to the building boom of the pre-2008 period. The Municipality has examined each case in detail, and itemised the cost of agreed works that still need to be fulfilled.

If the companies concerned are still trading they will have the option to immediately fulfil the agreement, or the bond funds will be seized so that the municipality can complete the outstanding work. This seems to be an obvious response and is the main purpose of the bond.

In the Canary Islands and Spain, there are many construction projects that remain incomplete. There are shopping centres, housing developments, roads and public buildings that have either been left abandoned at an early stage of work, or where the work has never started at all.

In all cases, a bond should have been lodged with the municipality to ensure that work is completed in time. However, in some cases, close fraternal links between developers and council officials ensure that drastic action, including confiscation of the bond to ensure that work is completed, is never taken, and many projects remain deep frozen in a kind of building 'limbo'.

We often hear of the need for rapid economic growth and the creation of employment opportunities, as well as building new homes. Maybe ensuring the completion of outstanding building projects, including building on land already earmarked for residential development, would be a welcome contribution to both the housing shortage, as well as providing employment opportunities.

How Does Your Garden Grow?

I have always enjoyed gardening. I don't mean the heavy-duty grind of growing vegetables, cutting hedges or mowing the lawn, but setting and growing plants that actually do something to lift the spirit. I like looking at, and admiring other people's gardens, visiting National Trust and other gardens in the UK and finding out more about particular plants that take my fancy.

Of course, when we moved to Spain, my gardening habits had to abruptly change. Initially, I was faced with a barren plot, and mostly covered with those dreaded reddish-brown outdoor tiles that the Spanish love so much.

I was fortunate, because there was a soil border where I could indulge my gardening fancies, and where a helpful neighbour encouraged me to install an underground watering system to ensure survival of most of my newly acquired plants during some of those blistering hot summer months in the Costa Blanca.

Later, when we moved to the Canary Islands, we had another problem. I was faced with the torment of living in an apartment with no outdoor space. The best that I could achieve was a few, mostly miserable looking pot plants on a table close to one of the few windows that had some light.

Although it was only planned as a temporary move, I think it was one of my most miserable experiences in Spain. How I craved for an outdoor space where I could grow a few plants. It was at that point that I realised how much plants and the opportunity for a little light gardening meant to me.

When we finally moved to our present home, we were fortunate in finding a property where we could have a garden with shrubs and maybe plant a small tree or two. Once again, the builders had unhelpfully laid most of the outdoor space with those wretched patio tiles, but these were quite easily removed and replaced with soil.

Beneath the soil we installed a watering system, and covered the soil with plastic sheeting to cut down on the weeding, and after a final layer of stones, we began to create our garden.

I am not a great lover of pots on patios, since we are surrounded by neighbours who, in an initial surge of gardening enthusiasm, buy a collection of those shiny blue, concrete pots, install a few beautiful plants and then forget to water them.

Many patios that I see are little more than graveyards for stumps of plants withering in these blue, shiny concrete planters. Whilst it is a huge generalisation, there is some truth in the fact that many Spanish people have little patience or understanding of plants and gardens. Their first inclination when they see bare soil is to concrete it over and lay yet more patio tiles.

Over the years that we have lived in Spain, I have learned not to grow plants that I used to love in the UK. It took me several years to finally understand the need to grow plants that suit local growing conditions. I don't mean cactus either; I don't mind some of the non-prickly, flowering varieties, but they are not really my favourite plants.

For me, this has meant moving away from growing azaleas, rhododendrons and camellias that were my favourites when I lived in Dorset. I now grow plants that include lavender, roses, anthuriums, aloe vera and even geraniums, which I always detested in the UK, to ensure all round colour and interest, as well as the ability to survive the excessive heat, dust and windy conditions that are now part of life in our Canarian garden.

Roses grow exceptionally well here, and I have several that are many years old and need to be replaced. However, when trying to find new roses in local garden centres I am told that they rarely stock roses, since they do not grow well in the Canary Islands. Well, they do grow well in our garden and although I feed them from time to time, I never have to spray them against black spot and other conditions that can be the bane of gardeners in the UK.

Although many of our UK and Irish friends understand and appreciate our small garden, the reaction from our Spanish friends and neighbours is usually one of amused tolerance, and with great concern expressed about what they perceive as a large water bill, as well as all the extra work that they think is necessary in maintaining even a small garden.

Too much is often made of national characteristics and cultural differences; however, for me, the love or hate of gardening is one of the big differences that I see between British and Spanish people. For me, it is time and money well spent. Our dog, Bella, enjoys helping me in the garden too.

The Mysterious Electrical Power Surge

Over the years that I have been writing 'Letters from the Atlantic', it has become something of a two-way exchange of views, and I am always grateful to those expats who are happy to share their experiences. 'Letters' is often based on questions and comments that I receive from expats in several countries who, like myself, are faced with challenging issues from time to time.

There are times when I think that I have slipped into an Alternative Universe, since no reasonable explanation or answer appears to be forthcoming. I suspect that many expats will know exactly what I mean as they deal with new laws, regulations, processes and bureaucracy in their newly adopted countries. I know from correspondence from readers that, on occasions, we all seem to battle against an issue that no one else seems to be aware of, or care about.

For me, one example is the mysterious electrical power surge. Often, whilst cooking a meal, working on the computer or watching television, the power will switch off for no apparent reason.

At first, I used to think that these were power cuts, but I have since learned that it is a power surge, since all the other homes around me still have electricity. At other times, our neighbour will find that his power switches off, whilst ours is still working.

I can understand why this may happen during a lightning storm, and even at times of heavy demand, such as meal times and excessive demand for air conditioning. However, when this occurs during quiet times and at night, I find this puzzling.

Anyone who knows anything about power surges will know that such surges can be very destructive. Unless appropriate gadgetry is provided to protect the circuit, appliances can be destroyed. This is the main purpose of the switch turning off when there is a power surge, but it can be so annoying.

It is particularly frustrating when using a computer, for instance, which is why I now protect these items with an uninterruptible power supply (UPS) box, which gives me just enough time to reset the power switch, or to correctly close down the computer and other delicate appliances.

Sometimes, this performance can go on for some time, in which case we sit in darkness (if at night) for a while, before attempting to switch the power on once again, in the hope that all has settled down. We then may go for several weeks before the problems begin again.

I have forgotten the number of times that I have left the house, boarded a flight somewhere, only to receive a text from the alarm company to report that the power in our house has failed. This then means that I have to call a very helpful friend, who has to go into our home to switch the power on again. I cannot leave it switched off because of food in the fridge and freezer. Often my friend will have to return to our house several times to restore the power, before it eventually settles down.

Over the years, I have mentioned the problem to neighbours, who nod ambiguously, and tell me that it happens to them too, but they don't seem at all concerned about it. I have reported it to the electricity company on several occasions, only for them either to deny that there is a problem, to suggest that it is my fault and that the electric circuits in our home should be checked, or that if they have to come out to check there will be a hefty inspection charge.

Some time ago, I asked an electrician to check that our circuitry was performing correctly, and I have also had the switch boxes replaced twice. On each occasion, I am told that all is working normally and that there is no problem inside or outside our property.

One electrician told me that properties receive power in groups of three installations and that the power fluctuation happens to all three properties at the same time, but not necessarily to all the properties in the same street. I am no expert on matters electrical, and this explanation mystifies me.

I am sure that by now, some readers will be identifying our home as the cause of the problem, but exactly the same thing happened in our previous home, an apartment just a few kilometres from our present home. Over the years that I have been on the island, no one so far has been able to satisfactorily explain why this happens and what can be done about it.

The response of most people is merely to switch the power back on again, which is not easy when you are travelling away from home. Surely, in these high-tech times, there is a simple way of levelling out power to prevent surges from reaching customers?

So, there we have it. If there are any electricians out there who can give me a reasonable and non-technical explanation of why this is happening, I would be most grateful. Similarly, I would also be interested to hear from other readers who may have the same problem and what they have done to correct it.

Life is Too Short to Stuff a Mushroom

I often think of that throwaway and impatient comment by the author, Shirley Conran, that "life's too short to stuff a mushroom". It is a quote that often occurs to me when I am confused, bewildered or reach a dead end in an argument that I am having with myself. I had one of these 'mushroom moments' a few days ago.

I've been uneasy about using the term 'expat' for many years. This confusion and conflict came to a head during the height of the migrant crisis when I began to see more clearly than ever before that there is no real difference between an 'expat' and an 'immigrant'.

As I have been writing a series of articles for 'expats' for some years, and published a book called 'Expat Survival', as well as running a popular website of the same name, it did seem an unnecessary complication and expense to change the title to 'Immigrant Survival', and so I left the issue on the 'back burner' to stew.

I am well aware that the subject of whether British 'expats' living in Spain, France, Italy etc. are expats or 'immigrants'. Personally, I am very happy to be known as a 'European Immigrant', for that is what I guess I am.

For me, the term 'expat' sounds colonial and temporary, whereas being an 'immigrant' sounds as if it is a long-term commitment, or even permanent. However, if we think about it, we are no different to the three million or so European immigrants currently living in the UK, yet we never refer to them as European, Spanish or French expats, do we?

I am aware that a debate over the subject can cause heated arguments over dinner, or drinks in the local 'expat' bar. If in doubt as to the true meaning, it is always a good idea to check the Oxford dictionary, which in this case defines an expat "as a person who lives outside their native country". It stems from the Latin "ex" meaning "out" and "patria" meaning native country.

So am I, and others like me, an 'expat' or an 'immigrant'. Personally, I am still confused…

Let us now consider the good people living in Boston, Lincolnshire, which has become a pinnacle of welcome for Polish and Romanian people living in the UK. Do the locals refer to them as 'expats' or 'immigrants'? Personally, I don't think I have ever heard the community being referred to as anything but 'immigrants', so why is it any different for myself and Brits living in the Canary Islands or the Costa Blanca?

By now, readers will probably think that I am being unnecessarily over pedantic about two simple words. No doubt I will also be accused of being 'politically correct', but words and definitions do matter, because they link to meaning, understanding and our subsequent attitudes to others.

If I use the word 'expat', am I referring to well off, and fortunate foreigners who have made a temporary move to a hot and sunny country, only to enjoy sipping gin and tonics on their terraces all day? I am certainly not referring to refugees from Syria or Africa fleeing for their lives, travelling across stormy seas with little more than the clothes that they are wearing.

However, are we not the same? Does it not really all boil down to a question of luck of where we happen to have been born and the opportunities that we have been given in life?

If we accept that immigrants are expats too, maybe it is a question of degree? Expats, in the traditional sense, usually have a choice of whether to return to the country of their birth or to stay in their adopted country, whilst many immigrants simply have no choice over their future.

Instead, maybe the term 'lucky immigrant' is a better term to describe those that have a choice in the matter, of moving for the sake of a better job, more money or a better lifestyle. This is in contrast to those immigrants who have no choice, but to attempt to escape poverty and persecution at whatever personal cost.

All this thinking really is hard work on a sunny afternoon, and in the end, I am not sure that it matters that much, as the two terms are not mutually exclusive. So, I have decided to continue to use the term 'expat', at least for the time being, mainly to avoid having my books reprinted. After all, sometimes life really is just too short to stuff a mushroom.

No Higher than a Palm Tree

A recent report that the London's Shard still has ten exclusive apartments that remain unsold, at a mere £50 million each, did not come as much of a surprise. These apartments are situated somewhere between the 53rd and 65th floors, so just imagine the difficulties if you wanted to pop out for a pizza and the lift wasn't working!

It takes all sorts and a great deal of money, of course, but I'm not sure that many people would fancy living in a building 224 metres tall. Imagine entertaining around 6000 visitors a day on the floors above the apartments; think of the sound of all those stilettoes clicking just above your head. Of course, the building was always intended to show off, and proudly proclaim that "we have the biggest one in the village", but whether it contributes anything really useful or worthwhile to the quality of life for Londoners, I guess depends upon the size of your wallet.

For many, at a time of a housing crisis for ordinary people in London, it is an extravagant and pointless waste of money; still, I guess the estate agents, developers and speculators have to do something with their time. According to some 'in the know', this expensive protrusion in the City is south of the river, and apparently anyone who is anyone wouldn't be seen anywhere south of the river anyway.

In contrast, let us now take a brief step away from a bustling London, to the clean air and tranquillity of the Canary Islands.

One of my local heroes is the Canarian artist, and Lanzarote's most famous son, César Manrique. He was not just an artist, but a painter, sculpture, architect, ecologist, planner of urban developments, as well as landscaper and gardener.

Manrique was fascinated by man's relationship with nature and became deeply concerned about the success and impact that mass tourism was having upon his beloved Canary Islands.

He witnessed the construction of some of the hideous hotels in the south of Tenerife and Gran Canaria, and was determined that the same violation would not happen to the island of Lanzarote. Fortunately, Manrique's fame and international acclaim meant that he was listened to.

Following a lengthy stay in New York, Manrique commented that "Man in New York is like a rat", and concluded that man is not well suited to an artificial environment. Feeling homesick, Manrique returned to Lanzarote, with an intention to turn Lanzarote into one of the more beautiful places on the planet. After his horror at seeing the twelve storey Gran Hotel that had been built in his home town, Arrecife, he declared that no building on the island (except church buildings) should be taller that a Canary palm tree (Phoenix Canariensis), which grows to between 15 to 20 metres in height.

Manrique became obsessive with surveying local architecture and the island's traditional culture, which he saw as the interface between nature and man.

Much to the chagrin of potential developers focussed upon mass tourism and profits from the exploitation of the island, Manrique's views prevailed and it is now impossible to visit Lanzarote without being aware of his overpowering influence. Tourism development does exist in several popular resorts, but in a controlled manner, and it is still difficult to find buildings that are taller than a palm tree.

Stepping back to London, I sometimes wonder what Manrique would have thought of the Shard, and enormous tower blocks housing hundreds of people within a heavily polluted city landscape.

Although his remedy of "no building being taller than a palm tree" would not work in London, New York or Hong Kong, where space is at a premium, I cannot help thinking that he was right, and that the population would be much happier in lower buildings with more space around them.

As for the apartments going for a song in the Shard, I think I'll pass on that one.

Going Electric

I was interested to read a recent report stating that electric cars are finally becoming popular in Europe. This is despite their slow adoption in the UK where motorists have been reluctant to buy battery-electric vehicles. For many years, buyers of new cars have been encouraged by governments to purchase diesel vehicles, blissfully unaware of some of their environmental dangers.

Many motorists became convinced that they were the ideal alternative to petrol models; it seems that they were wrong. At last, Europe's collective mind-set is beginning to change with sales of battery-powered cars growing by 38 per cent in the first quarter of 2017. 32,627 cars were registered in European Union countries, Norway and Switzerland, when compared to 23,703 in the first quarter of 2016.

I get quite attached to cars. Over time, many have become like old friends; after all, the better ones have provided convenience, safety and reliability over many years. Personally, I see little need to change a car simply because of its age or to keep up with the neighbours.

One of our cars is a Hyundai Getz, which was one of our first purchases when we moved to Spain's Costa Blanca 15 years ago. It has been a remarkable little car, requiring only the minimum basic attention, together with occasional re-spraying of parts of its bodywork as a result of sun damage.

We tend to rather cherish it nowadays, as it became our home and reassurance during one traumatic week when we moved from the Costa Blanca to the Canary Islands. It safely transported us during the three-day ferry crossing from Cadiz, with two dogs, essential personal belongings and the precious laptop computer with which we would launch the first edition of a new English language newspaper on the island. During those first few days on the island, our little car became a refuge from the outside world of chaos, confusion and builders.

Fifteen years on, although having been around the clock at least once, our little Getz is still going strong. Living on an island, travelling huge distances is simply not possible. Since most of my work is completed at home, I don't have long distances to travel to work either. I guess if I am faced with a major expense, the time will come when I have to reluctantly say goodbye to the Getz, so what will my choice be? Petrol, diesel or electric?

Personally, I am all in favour of an electric car. Despite a number of discussions and arguments that I have had with the 'petrol is best' brigade, for me, an electric car will win hands down. It's amazing how many motorists become very angry when discussing this issue, with many determined to rubbish electric vehicles at all costs, and often with arguments that bear very little relationship to facts.

Yes, I know all about the very expensive and poor life of battery issues, restricted mileage and all the rest. The only one that slightly bothers me is the lack of sound when the vehicle is moving. I see this as a major safety issue, and I really would want a vehicle that made a noise when moving. I don't really mind what the sound is; maybe an Abba song is a possibility? A distinctive sound of some kind is essential to warn pedestrians that a car is likely to hit them unless they move out of the way. I guess that is an easy problem to fix.

The Canary Islands, and the Spanish Costas, benefit from boundless energy from the sun, and in the Canary Islands, in particular, we have sufficient wind and wave energy to meet the needs of most consumption of electricity on the islands. The missing factor is a lack investment and insight into the potential of these renewable resources. Of course, as usual, the oil companies and politics get into the way of such common-sense developments, and most of us are left with no alternative, but to use a petrol, or even worse, a diesel vehicle.

Of course, there is another snag, and that is the issue of charging points. We are told that high speed charging points are popping up all over Europe and that a huge amount of money is being spent on building such networks. I spotted one charging point for the Mayor's electric vehicle outside the Town Hall of a municipality in Lanzarote recently. Hopefully, this is a sign of things to come throughout the islands.

In my excitement, I downloaded an app on my smartphone, which is designed to tell me of the whereabouts of all charging points on the islands, as well as the one closest to my home. Sadly, the nearest one is on the Island of Madeira, which would involve a lengthy ferry trip. I guess I'll stick with the Getz for now.

The TV Sports Package

It has been a strange week, as far as the Internet goes anyway. For many expats living in Spain and the Canary Islands, the vagaries, confusion and general unreliability of the established telephone company, Movistar (or Telefonica as it used to be called) tend to both mystify and amuse on some days, but generally add to life's anger and frustration on others.

Some years ago, as a newly arrived expat and newspaper reporter in the Costa Blanca, it was one of my jobs to follow the latest 'Telefonica Story'. It was both an eye catching and eye watering responsibility, since I witnessed the distress of many expats at first hand. This was a time when mobile phone and data coverage was poor, if non-existent, and many newly arrived expats were desperate to be able to call the folks back home, as well as carry out banking and other business activities.

I covered news stories ranging from the sick and elderly who desperately needed a telephone connection to be able to communicate with the hospital or doctor, with one case of an elderly woman who was refused a connection to 'the pole' simply, because it was just one metre outside the specified distance.

I stood in queues with other angry expats outside the Telefonica offices for many hours, clutching the precious 'bread ticket' waiting for the latest allocation of phone numbers, before the door was firmly closed at 13.00 hours for siesta. Would it be my turn to be seen or would I have to return again tomorrow?

I have witnessed grown men cry with anger, disgust and despair. It was not uncommon for newly arrived expats to wait for two years or longer before they could get a telephone connection. The Telefonica office itself was a den of misery, with queues of expats stretching to well outside the building, with desperate people begging for a telephone contract at any price. I witnessed the offhand and often cruel dismissal by Telefonica 'jobsworths', a speciality that they were very good at.

In fairness, the successor organisation with its friendlier name of Movistar has improved over the last ten years or so, but I sometimes wonder if this is only surface deep, since there still appears to be a huge way to go to drag this stumbling dinosaur into something close to the 21st Century. Generally, I am not a believer in the privatisation of essential services, such as electricity, water and telephones, but Telefonica/Movistar offers a clear case for radical reform. Certainly, it makes the UK's BT look like almost angelic.

Fifteen years on, I still regularly receive complaints from expats about Movistar's standards of customer service, which often continue to be off-hand and self-serving. The 'Customer Care' staff seem much more interested in selling Internet television sports packages than they are in dealing with a problem.

Of course, customer support staff are paid on commission, and who can blame their attempts to collect a few more euros in their pay packets, but at what price to the consumer? Surely, someone should have pointed out to them long ago the difference between offering customers a service to rectify a problem instead of trying to sell them a product that they don't want or is simply inappropriate? It is really frustrating to be asked if I would like a Sports TV package when I cannot even get an Internet signal.

For the last two years or so, we have been tempted with the offer of a fast, fibre optic Internet connection in our village. The suits have been out, held impressive, lengthy promotional meetings for the press, accompanied by those dreaded PowerPoint presentations. Two years on, we are still waiting. We have seen roads dug up, channels made, and pipes and cables installed. We have even seen a cable laid to our gate and into the Movistar box that sits patiently outside. Are we connected? No.

A few days ago, we received an automated telephone call from Movistar, cheerfully explaining that the work was complete and that if we would care to telephone the Movistar Customer Care line, we could order our new fibre optic connection. We were excited, telephoned the Customer Care line (which, is not true, because they really couldn't care less unless you buy a sports TV package).

The woman I spoke to, took my details, bank account information and confidently assured me that the fibre optic connection would be made available to us during the afternoon that same day! This was amazing and, sensing my doubts, even checked again with the engineer that this would happen. It was confirmed, and on this occasion, I was even tempted to buy the sports TV package, just to please her, but I stopped myself just in time.

Two days later, we are still waiting for super-fast fibre optic broadband to be connected. I telephoned to check, but after trying to get through to a busy line for most of the day, was eventually told that it was not available and that I would be informed when this is possible, maybe in a month or two. I was clearly the victim of agreeing to a contract just to generate a few more euros commission for the member of the customer service team, and with no possibility of the order being fulfilled as promised.

To add a further insult, we no longer have an Internet connection of any description. When I call Customer Care once again to complain, you can imagine my response to the offer for a sports TV package!

Health, Happiness and Compassion

The
Canary
Islander

Sugar is So Taxing

I was shocked to read this week that the most obese children in the world are in the United States of America, Mexico <u>and the Canary Islands,</u> which is seen as a micro culture representing the highest obesity levels in Europe. The Canary Islands are the first region in Spain to follow the recommendations of the World Health Organisation that a 20 per cent increase in the price of 'guilty products' will help to save lives by raising awareness.

These statistics are frightening and I recall writing about this issue when we first moved to the Canary Islands. I could not understand why, in the village where we lived, there were so many grossly overweight people and, in particular, children.

As well as enormously overweight adults, it was also clear that many adults were suffering from mobility and joint problems, leg ulcers, diabetes and many other ailments associated with obesity. There were at that time, and still are, many children who demonstrate acute obesity levels from a very young age.

The Government of the Canary Islands has announced a new tax that is designed to save lives. The new sugar tax will be applied to food and drink that contain sugar, in an effort to persuade residents to reduce their consumption of sugary drinks and food.

Of course, there are always pros and cons in arguments related to taxation, with one side claiming that the tax will assist in improving health outcomes, whilst the other side talk about taxing those who can least afford it.

In a wet and cold climate, I can understand why many children and teenagers will prefer to stay indoors to play computer games, but in the Canarian climate there can be no such excuses. There are plenty of outdoor activities easily and freely available to encourage children to participate in an outdoor and physically active life.

There are indoor and outdoor swimming pools, football pitches and a well-equipped sports centre in the village, and as it is close to the sea, there are always beach activities available. Many Canarian families have the use of small fishing boats, which can also be a strenuous physical activity.

Of course, in these days of political correctness, very few people face the real issues of being overweight, which is that we eat too much of the wrong kind of food and drink, or simply devour too much of everything.

Instead, many 'experts' trot out platitudes that the issue may be due to "genetic reasons", but I doubt that the early settlers of the islands and the ancestors of many local people, the Guanches, were as grossly overweight as current generations. Being "big boned" is another excuse that I often hear, as well as thyroid problems, which can be a problem for some older people, but is quite rare in children.

It seems that excuses are always freely available when it comes to obesity, because many of us are simply addicted to sugar.

On occasions when I am passing the local school at the end of the school day, I see parents waiting for their young offspring to appear from the classrooms. The first thing that most parents do after greeting their child, is to hand over a large bag of crisps, sweets or a giant bottle of cola.

Teenagers in our local shop can be seen after school focussed upon buying super large bottles of fizzy drinks, chocolate, biscuits and cakes. In the supermarket, trolleys are laden with bottles of fizzy drinks, biscuits, cakes and sweets, but I rarely see equally generous helpings of fruit and vegetables being loaded into trolleys.

Current statistics tell us that 1.5 million Canarian residents are overweight, which includes 760,000 who are classified as obese. This, in turn, contributes to the highest death rate from heart attack in all of Spain. The new sugar tax is being criticised by many, yet Canary Islands' residents are leading the world for all the wrong dietary reasons.

Education is also important here too, since many Canarian residents need help to encourage them to eat and drink more healthy options. Many local people simply do not know that processed foods include hidden added sugars, such as glucose or fructose, which are found in soups, yogurts and soft drinks.

It is hoped that, given time, this new sugar tax will help to change attitudes and that these appalling statistics will be reduced.

This Cruel Sea

It is true that less tourists return home alive than have set off for their holiday in the Canary Islands. This disturbing fact is not one that the tourist industry will thank me for highlighting this week, but it is time that the stark facts are raised once again and that holidaymakers are alerted to the potential risks of a holiday in the Canary Islands, and other popular tourist destinations.

The Canary Islands are a wonderful place for a holiday, but it is best not to return home in a coffin. We have the best climate in the world; each of the seven inhabited islands are unique and offer a range of activities and experiences that will enrich the spirit of even the most hardened and cynical traveller. The problem for tourists is not the islands, but the Atlantic Ocean.

Ours is a cold and cruel sea. It is deceptive in its appeal, but it is no Mediterranean Sea. Many tourists forget this and quickly succumb to the delights of this turbulent water. Its many charms lull the unsuspecting tourist into a false sense of security with its frothy and inviting appeal to swimmers, surf boarders, wind surfers, but those with a true knowledge of the Atlantic Ocean will be only too well aware of its rapidly changing moods and boiling anger that erupts from time to time.

As I write this, statistics from Real Federación Española de Salvamento y Socorrismo are worrying. There have already been 35 drownings in the first half of 2017, which is more than the same period in 2016, which places the Canary Islands at the top of a very disturbing league table, with most of these casualties being tourists. Statistics published in 2015 indicate that one tourist drowns every six days in the Canary Islands, a record that is one of the worst in Spain.

The shock of very cold water, swimming after a heavy meal, after drinking alcohol or taking drugs are some of the reasons for these individual tragedies. Cardiac arrest in the sea is not unusual, since it is the result of the shock of cold water, even in temperatures of around 25 degrees.

The water around these islands rarely exceeds 24 degrees, even in the hottest periods of the year; it is not just freezing water that is a danger to swimmers. Despite the temptations to cool off after a day in the sun, swimmers can get into difficulties in as short a time as five minutes.

Many tourists forget that high winds, rough seas and treacherous currents are the main reasons for many drownings that take place each year. A strong undertow and unpredictable rip currents are also a grave danger to swimmers. They are unseen and unpredictable, catch swimmers without warning and carry them a considerable distance out to sea.

Rough seas around our beautiful coastline can also be a danger for unsuspecting walkers, which may occur even in what appears to be good and settled weather. It depends what mood the Atlantic is in, and freak waves have sometimes swept walkers out to sea.

Some of these issues were brought home to me last weekend when I visited one of our popular, local beaches. It was a beautiful, yet stormy morning and the red warning flags were flying. Despite this, there were many swimmers in the sea, together with several surfboarders.

I spotted two lifeguards urging swimmers to come to the shore for safety, which most obeyed. These swimmers were then directed to a safer part of the beach. However, several swimmers, including the surfboarders, continued to ignore the lifeguards.

It is this attitude of bravado and ignorance that is behind many swimming tragedies, and it is hard to legislate against foolishness. Sadly, it is also these attitudes that place the safety of lifeguards and other members of the emergency services at risk. Despite the best efforts of the islands' government, the municipalities and the emergency services, swimming tragedies continue to occur far too frequently.

The Work-Life Balance

Getting the work-life balance right is not easy for many people, and for many juggling with earning enough to pay the rent or mortgage, food and other bills, there is often very little choice in the amount of free time available. Time to spend with families and friends is important, and I often admire the Spanish tradition of putting family life first whenever possible.

The Spanish Minister for Tourism and Technology was recently musing about the impact of technological changes upon society, and suggested that a three-day weekend was almost inevitable. The Minister spoke about fast moving technological developments in communication, public administration and education, and the 51.2 million mobile phones that are in use throughout Spain.

With 40 million people having ready access to a mobile Internet connection, more people could work from home or 'on-the-go'. He went on to say that this approach to work would have positive effects on health, productivity and public spending.

The Minister raises some good points, and his ideas are not new, since many claim that the traditional employment structure is bad for health. Time spent with family and friends is the most important part of life, and with work being the means with which we pay for it.

In many ways, this 'flexible' and more relaxed style of living and working in the Canary Islands has been operating for many years.

Very few shops, and certainly no offices or banks, are open on a Saturday afternoon. The few shops that do open (unless they are situated in commercial centres or tourist areas) close their doors at lunch time on Saturday, and may or may not reopen on Monday morning. Many Canarians take Monday off work, which is why shopping, banking and visiting Town Halls is never a good idea on Mondays.

Fiestas and family life are very important in the Canary Islands. Most weeks are punctuated by a different fiesta in towns and villages across the islands. Often those living in neighbouring municipalities feel the urge to join in too, and close their doors early on the day before the big event to allow time to prepare food, shop and to dress up for the big day.

Schools close at the end of June for the traditional long, summer holiday and reopen again in mid-September. In many ways, this is necessary, because of the excessive heat in Spain and the Canary Islands at this time of the year; few classrooms enjoy the luxury of air conditioning. It is a time when children and their families can enjoy a long summer break together, and it is taken very seriously.

For some children, sports, language and summer camps are an option, which some busy parents take full advantage of. However, these facilities do not come cheap and for many families the only option is for grandparents to share the load and for parents take time off work to be with their offspring.

As a result, legal, financial, postal and most other services grind to a halt, since no one ever seems to consider staggering holiday entitlement or to appoint reserve and back up staff to cover the shortfall of workers.

Then there is the dreaded August 15th. This is the day when almost everything closes down (except in the tourist areas) for at least two weeks, and possibly more. Most of us are longing to get back to normal, which will happen sometime in mid-September, but definitely by October!

Despite such inconveniences, Spanish and Canarian workers do work very hard and for long hours. Most shops and offices open from about 08.00am, and closure at 10.00pm is not unusual, particularly in commercial centres. Most small shops close at around 1.30pm for the traditional siesta, and open their doors again at around 4.00pm. This is the time when Spanish workers traditionally eat their main meal of the day, followed by a siesta.

However, in more recent times and with increasingly long distances to travel to work, few workers make it home for a family meal at this time of the day. The midday break is important, because of the heat, and it is time to cool down and relax away from the heat of the day.

Many Spanish and Canarian workers have two jobs, which again is why the mid-afternoon break is useful for workers to get from one job to another. I know a number of shop workers who start work at 08.00am, work until the siesta and then hastily drive to the tourist areas where they begin their evening shifts as waiters and bar staff, and usually finish their shift at 11.00pm or much later if it is bar work.

A revised working structure for the working week has been trialled in parts of the United States and Sweden, but it is unclear whether it will ever become a reality for Spain. However, the Spanish Government is giving serious consideration to removing the siesta, starting work later and finishing the day earlier.

Animals Need Our Help Too

It has been a distressing week in Gran Canaria. A major fire broke out in the heavily forested centre of the island, which is in an area that we often visit. It is a region that few tourists can be bothered to visit, for which residents are grateful, since not only is it an area of spectacular natural beauty, but an area of peace and tranquillity. It is well away from the pressures of the modern world, the sun beds, fast food restaurants and bars in the busy tourist area in the south of the island.

Not only the Gran Canaria fire, but many other news stories have been particularly distressing over the last few weeks. Tragedies, such as the Grenfell Tower fire, flooding in Bangladesh, horrendous hurricanes in the Caribbean, volcanic eruptions in Italy and the horrors of 'ethnic cleansing' in Myanmar, have made an impact upon all but the most cold and detached personalities.

As we watch these horrors unfold in faraway places in the comfort of our own living rooms, it is often difficult to identify with the pain and suffering that ordinary people experience when faced with such disasters.

Although, I understand that the suffering and welfare of people come first, I know that I am not the only one to be distressed about animals caught up in such disasters. There is rarely any mention of animals caught up in flooding, fire and other tragedies that appear on our television screens, and little is ever reported.

It seems that animals suddenly become invisible during times of crisis, yet as all animal lovers will know, they have become part of our lives and highly important. Dogs, cats, horses, donkeys, birds and reptiles, as well as farm animals often perish in horrendous circumstances during these periods of exceptional tragedy, and it seems that they are forgotten and left behind during the pressure of rescue efforts.

This point was brought home to me this week whilst reporting on the forest fire, which quickly got out of control on the island where I live. The fire spread quickly and destroyed many hectares of land, involving five municipalities. A number of villages and many people were evacuated.

Thanks to the brave and selfless efforts of the emergency services, it appears that only one life was lost. The woman who died was an expat, originally from Sweden, who had made her life on our beautiful island. She refused to leave her home, preferring to stay and look after her animals. Her charred body was later discovered outside her home. One can only imagine her terror, as she was consumed by the flames.

It is often difficult to identify with the hundreds and thousands of people in distress that appear on our television screens, but it is the distress of small groups and individuals that help us to understand their pain and suffering. For me, it was the dying moments of this terrified woman that has stayed in my mind. I did not know her, but the fact that she bothered to stay behind to care for her animals tells me a lot about her compassion and humanity, and I suspect that she is someone who I would have liked.

Spain and the Canary Islands are often rightly criticised for attitudes to animals, which can often appear casual, uncaring and exploitative. Over the years that I have lived in Spain and the Canary Islands, there have been many times when I have wished that we had the equivalent of the UK's RSPCA, PDSA and many other dedicated animal charities helping to protect animals in Spain. Sadly, this is not the case, and much is left to hard-stretched police, as well as dedicated individuals, to help to relieve the plight of animals suffering in this country.

There is some good news to help to soothe the rawness of this latest tragedy on the island for animals that need veterinary help. The Veterinary Department of the University of Las Palmas is currently helping animals that have suffered, but escaped from the fire at a centre in the town of San Mateo. Volunteers from the College of Vets at the University of Las Palmas are offering a 24-hour service to help these animals. Dogs and cats can be taken directly to a central animal point for care and attention.

It is often said that a society can be judged by its attitude towards animals. I have always believed this to be true, and in these polarised and often selfish times, it is heart-warming that the needs of animals are also being considered following a tragedy that has affected all precious life.

Money, Money, Money

The
Canary
Islander

Avoid Currency Exchange 'Rip Offs'

I know that many British expats living in Europe are feeling very anxious about the pound-euro exchange rate at the present time. Although not unexpected, Brexit has started a period of considerable financial uncertainty for expats, which will take some time to resolve.

Many expats rely upon an income from the UK, be it a salary or a company or state pension, and even a small difference in the exchange rate will make a considerable difference to their standard of living. Gone are those heady days when one pound would buy 1.50 euro; even at that time many of us realised that the pound was grossly overvalued, and that a day of reckoning would happen in the future. Even so, it was nice whilst it lasted.

At the time of writing, commenting about exchange rates is always difficult, since this article may be read many weeks or months after it is written, and the pound appears to be heading for parity with the euro. Some financial 'experts' are already claiming that the pound will shortly be worth less than the euro, whilst others are claiming that the pound will revert to its usual 'high' after a year or two, or when Brexit is finally settled.

Frankly, it is all guess work and we may as well ask, "How long is a piece of string?" In reality, no one knows, so let us deal with issues that expats and holidaymakers are facing here and now, and let us make the most of the pounds that we have.

Holidaymakers and expats are already complaining that they are receiving only one euro for one pound at airport currency exchange desks. Frankly, my view is that if they are foolish enough to exchange their pounds at the airport just before they leave for their holiday, they deserve a poor exchange rate.

Airport currency exchange rates have to include charges for their fancy booths and shops, trained staff and smart uniforms; one is paying for convenience and this is the penalty for leaving it so late. The more astute travellers arrange their overseas currency long before they leave the UK, maybe through an online currency exchange dealer, their local bank or the Post Office. I suggest that travellers use none of these services, and that many more competitive services are now available that will leave more currency in their pockets.

Today, at the time of writing and after speaking to some holidaymakers who were complaining to me that they received less than parity at a currency booth in Gatwick Airport, I managed to get 1.12 euros for one pound by using an app on my mobile phone when I went shopping today, as well as drawing cash out of a local ATM.

For transactions in Europe, I usually use a debit card provided by a 'fintech' company called Revolut for many of my currency transactions, or a debit card provided through a superb UK banking operation called Starling Bank. There are several others to consider, such as Monzo and Monese that offer similar services that should be considered. All of these companies provide a mobile phone app and a prepaid debit card that you can use to pay for goods and services whilst on holiday or to draw cash out of overseas ATMs.

Instead of paying a fancy commission to one of the airport currency exchange booths, holidaymakers and expats can obtain currency at wholesale rates through the use of these services.

If living in Europe, I recommend that British expats seriously consider opening an account with Revolut or Monese. If maintaining an address in the UK, go for Starling Bank or Monzo for the best currency exchange rates. Another app based bank, N26, which I also use, is based in Germany and offers full banking protection. Although currently only offering a euro-based account, it is planning to offer a sterling account, as well as a euro account in the near future, and is certainly well worth keeping an eye on.

All of these accounts can be opened through your iPhone or Android device. They have certainly made my financial life overseas easier to manage, and I am no longer ripped off by the large currency exchange services.

Making Money in the Canary Islands

Some time ago, I received publicity material for the Canary Islands' edition of the board game, Monopoly. For those of you who are not familiar with the game, I can assure you that it is a very pleasant all-islands version of the popular board game, but relevant to the delights of the Canary Islands, rather than the smog and stresses of London, which most British players will be familiar with.

Have you ever played Monopoly? Some of you may well groan at the memory of bitter squabbles and arguments when losing, whilst for others it may bring happy memories of playing with family and friends, whilst setting you on a path to be a successful entrepreneur. I used to play it, but it was not a game that I was very keen on, or really understood.

I do remember being unhappy unless I managed to get the little dog as a playing piece, as well as being teased, because I was never interested in buying the 'posh' London estates in Mayfair and Park Lane, because I much preferred the cosier properties in Old Kent Road. Needless to say, I never did become a successful businessman and much preferred the game of Scrabble instead.

Despite my lack of enthusiasm for the game, it has been remarkably successful over the years. For those who are more used to playing video games, I should explain that Monopoly is a game of chance; a board game whereby players roll two six-sided dice to move around the board, buying and selling properties. Players collect rent from their opponents, with the charming aim of trying to drive opponents into bankruptcy.

The game was invented by an American woman, an anti-monopolist called Elizabeth Magie, in 1903 as a way to demonstrate a capitalist economy. It was intended to demonstrate that an economy that rewards the creation of wealth is better than one in which monopolists operate under less constraints. There is also a more sinister underpinning to the game in that it is designed to promote the work of Henry George and his theories of taxation.

One story about the game that I particularly like, is that in 1941, the British Secret Service approached the British manufacturer of the game, John Waddington, to create a special edition for World War 2 prisoners captured by the Nazis. Compasses, maps, real money and other items that might come in useful for escaping were hidden inside these games. These 'special editions' were distributed to prisoners of war by British secret service agents disguised as charity workers.

In 1991, Hasbro bought Parker Brothers and its interests in Monopoly and happily went on to allow multiple licensing of the game across the world. As well as board games, a variety of spin offs appeared including a live TV game show, computer and video games, gambling versions for slot machines, on line versions, films, tournaments, and even a World championship event.

There are already a number of published local Spanish editions for Ibiza, Granada, the Basque

Country and Cantabria, as well as special editions celebrating sports teams such as Barcelona Football Club or Real Madrid, among others. According to the company, this special edition was selected because of the Canary Islands' "incredible natural environment, its enormous wealth and cultural variety and its international relevance at a tourist level".

The Canary Islands edition of the game is published by a British company, Winning Moves, and is produced as a bilingual Spanish-English version. It has the support of three large companies that operate throughout the archipelago: Fred Olsen Express, Lopesan Group and Cajasiete. The game maintains the aesthetics and rules of the traditional game, so should be enjoyed by tourists and residents alike.

Over the years, the game has been vastly improved, but maybe the new Canary Islands' edition could include the large Canary Mastiff dog as one of its playing pieces? Monopoly is still going from strength to strength. Anyone for a game?

Where There's Money, There's Muck

Sewage is a subject that most people avoid talking and thinking about, but it is at the very core of human and animal existence. Whatever our status and power in society, this is the one thing that we all have in common and society deals with it as best it can.

Over the last few years, the Canary Islands have become an increasingly popular destination. Rightly so, since few places can offer such an equitable climate throughout the year. However, this popularity has not come without cost, and the more popular resorts on the largest islands have been both shocked and embarrassed by the consequences of untreated sewage that has found its way into the sea.

Rather like climate change deniers, there are many working within local governments, the tourist industry and major hotel chains who regard the 'green bloom' that has appeared on the sea at the islands' most popular beaches as simply a trivial irritation rather than facing the fact that the green bloom is the result of algae feasting on the excessive nutrients produced by raw sewage pumped into the sea. The green bloom can cause skin disorders and other health problems if you swim in it. This problem is a combination of excess sewage, still water and the heat of the summer months, and is well recognised by many scientists, academics and health workers.

Of course, this issue varies according to each island and the seriousness with which the authorities deal with the matter. I won't identify the 'sinning' islands in this 'Letter', but the information has already been published in local newspapers, and much to the annoyance of the 'deniers'. Several islands treat nearly all of their raw sewage, whilst others pump the vast majority of its sewage directly into the sea, and then wonder why, with increasing numbers of tourists, there is a problem.

Another challenge is the sludge that is created following the treatment of sewage. On the island of Gran Canaria, 70,000 tons of sewage sludge is produced each year, which costs the island four million euros a year to deposit this sludge in environmental centres. The island is currently considering an imaginative and environmentally friendly way of dealing with sewage sludge that will also create a considerable economic advantage.

A recent study has concluded that it is possible to generate a compost from the sludge that could be used in agriculture, saving up to 38% of water in the process of composting. This can be used as a fertiliser, and performs as well as conventional fertilisers. Current studies show that compost made in Gran Canaria is more balanced and stable than imported compost, as well as avoiding restrictions on importing agricultural products to the island.

Although tourism is very important to all the islands, we must not forget that the islands' agricultural industry has always been and continues to be essential. Growing fruit and vegetables for export provides a significant income, but the costs of importing fertiliser are high. The use of locally produced compost would also be an economic advantage, since it is estimated that the agricultural industry would save more than seven million euros, which is the cost of importing twelve million kilos of fertiliser to the island each year. Farmers would also benefit from the reduction in price of water for irrigation.

It is imaginative thinking such as this that will help to ease the many problems that an ever-increasing tourist population is creating on the islands. In future, let us hope that tourists will not only be welcome for the money that they spend in the Canary Islands, but also for the waste that they leave behind.

Memories, Nightmares and Dreams

The Canary Islander

Typewriter Terror

The phone rang; it was a colleague in Las Palmas telling me that the police were in the middle of a response to a potential terrorist incident in the city. A suspect package had been placed in front of the door to the garage of the central offices of the National Police on the island. The building was sealed off, traffic was prevented from entering the road, and anti-terrorist officers arrived to assess the potential danger of the package. These officers quickly discovered that this was a false alarm, and since the suspicious package turned out to contain nothing more lethal than an antique typewriter, the panic was over.

Two days later I found myself browsing in a charity shop that I occasionally visit. I always find it fascinating to browse through old books, records and maybe find a technological treasure from the past, such as an old radio or ancient camera. This time, I spotted a typewriter, an old Olympia, sitting proudly on an antique desk. It looked in remarkably good condition, and one that I guessed was made in the mid 1960s.

This machine brought back a flood of memories of my father bringing his portable typewriter home from work each day and patiently teaching me to type when I was still at primary school. In more recent times, I have been thankful for computers, tablets and all the other gadgetry that make life so much simpler. Did I really want to use a typewriter again?

Later that morning, I returned to the shop and asked for a sheet of paper to test the typewriter. Amazingly, all the keys worked, and the type was clear and aligned. It felt smooth and accurate to the touch, which was surprising for a 50-year-old machine; it had clearly been well looked after. It also came with a very smart protective case. As I handed over the ten euros asking price, I asked the man looking after the shop to tell more about where it had come from. He told me that it had come to the shop as part of a house clearance following the death of "an important man" several years ago.

The typewriter had been forgotten and only recently put on display. He wouldn't tell me any more about the original owner of the typewriter, and seemed pleased when I stopped asking questions and left. I returned to my car, pleased with my purchase, although it was much heavier than I remembered. I was also intrigued by the response to my questions, and felt that there was much more to discover.

It was when cleaning the machine that I found an old sticker in the case with the name of the shop that had originally supplied it. The sticker included a phone number, which was in a different pattern of numbers currently used. It was not too hard to track down the modern version of the number and I decided to call it. Although it was doubtful that the shop would still be in business, I remembered that many businesses in the Canary Islands are passed through many generations, even though the original trade may have changed. To my surprise, the telephone number worked, and a man answered.

The man listened patiently to my story about the typewriter and told me that his father had owned the shop, but had died some years ago. As well as selling typewriters, his father had also serviced them. Although the current business no longer sold typewriters, the son had kept some records; did I know the serial number of the machine? Fortunately, I had already predicted that I would be asked this question and had written it down. The son took a note of the number and promised that he would call me back "mañana". My heart sank when he said this, since "mañana' is often a polite way of saying 'never'.

Two days later, I received a telephone call. True to his word, the son had checked his father's records, and found the serial number of my typewriter, the date of sale and the servicing that it had received. This time, the son was quite animated and told me that the machine had belonged to someone important, who had died. As I was British, he doubted that I would appreciate the significance, and asked if I would like to sell the typewriter back to him.

He wouldn't tell me who it had belonged to, and I began to imagine that he would be quoting the words "data protection", which is the current way of denying reasonable information requests. I thanked him for his trouble, but declined the offer, as I wanted to keep the typewriter.

Even more intriguing was when I tried to buy a new ribbon for the typewriter. When the ribbon arrived from the UK, it would not fit. I contacted the supplier, who assured me that it was the correct ribbon for an Olympia. He was puzzled as to why it would not fit and asked me to send him photos of the typewriter and the old ribbon spools. His reply was even more puzzling, since it seems that my Olympia typewriter is in fact an Olivetti. He is a typewriter expert and had not come across this issue before and suggested that the labels had been switched at some stage in its life, but could not explain the serial number that related to an Olympia.

My imagination began to work overtime; was it all part of a complicated plot, with a switched identity of both its owner and the typewriter? It certainty left me wondering even more about its history and that of its previous owner.

I always appreciate a good mystery, and I also now have a rather splendid typewriter that I will use from time to time. I will always be fascinated by the story behind it, even though I have yet to discover who the "important person" was and why the identity of my typewriter was changed.

As far as the original news story that started my week is concerned, I am still wondering why an antique typewriter was left outside the central police office. After all, does anyone use a typewriter nowadays?

Wells Are For Life and Not to Hide Corpses

Many people do not realise that the Spanish Civil War of 1936 actually began in the Canary Islands. Francisco Franco was General Commandant of the Canary Islands, who was based in Las Palmas de Gran Canaria. It was here that Franco plotted his strategy, well away from the rest of Spain, before he headed to the Spanish Peninsular. It was under his watch that Spain became divided into two factions: 'Republican' and 'Loyalists'.

The Spanish Civil War began on July 18, 1936, as a revolt by right-wing Spanish military officers in Spanish Morocco that spread to Peninsular Spain. Franco broadcast his message from the Canary Islands, which called for all army officers to join the uprising and overthrow Spain's leftist Republican government.

The Republicans and the Nationalists secured their territories by executing thousands of suspected political opponents. The horrors of the Spanish Civil War are still very raw in Spain and the Canary Islands, and continue to have a significant impact upon the loyalties and divisions of all the islands; the scars of which remain today.

Recently, archaeologists excavated a well in Tenoy in Gran Canaria, finding the bones of at least 12 people, including a skull with a gunshot wound. This was one of the places where local people experienced the horrors and repression of the Spanish Civil War.

The old well of Tenoy, in the municipality of Arucas, is one of the places where 140 inhabitants of the north of Gran Canaria disappeared in March 1937. It is believed that these victims were assassinated after spending months in one of Franco's concentration camps for being loyal to the Second Republic. The project has so far found half a million human bones, a Republican coin, buckles, soles of traditional shoes and ammunition.

Some of the evidence comes from a direct and tragic account of the incident from a Galdar resident, who had been shot at the entrance to the Tenoy well. His friend rescued him and moved him to a safe house. Over the years, the contents of this well became buried with tons of mud and lost memories.

Other wells are also being searched on the island, including Llano de las Brujas, where 24 bodies were recovered. In addition, the search for people missing during the Franco dictatorship led to mass graves in the cemeteries of Vegueta and Sima de Jinamar.

The excavations of wells on the island reveal some of the horrors of the Spanish Civil War. It tells the story of how local residents of Gran Canaria who opposed the ruling class were often placed in concentration camps, killed and their bodies hidden in wells.

As one descendent, who has spent her life searching for the body of her murdered father, has so eloquently put it, "Wells are not meant to hide corpses. Wells are to give life. I want to put the bones of my father where they should be, in the cemetery". It is a tragic history, but maybe finding some of the missing bodies and giving them an appropriate burial will help to ease some of the pain and provide closure for their families.

A Beacon of Culture

As regular readers may remember, I started playing the violin again last year. In fact, I became so enthusiastic that I started teaching myself to play the viola and cello as well.

Sometimes it is a painful and painstaking process, and I would not inflict my efforts upon any listener. However, I do enjoy listening to stringed instruments, and in particular, being played by those who really do know how to make their instruments sing.

Last week, I was fortunate to be able to attend a concert given by the Gran Canaria Philharmonic Orchestra. Most tourists, and indeed many residents, remain unaware that we have our own world class orchestra on this island.

There are regular concerts advertised and I can highly recommend making the effort to travel to the Alfredo Kraus Auditorium in Las Palmas for the evening; it is a delightful and impressive experience.

I particularly enjoy visiting the Alfredo Kraus Auditorium in Las Palmas. It has often been described as "A Beacon of Culture", which it is in so many symbolic ways. Looking at the impressive building as it stands on Las Canteras beach is just a start.

For me, the true magic begins inside the building when looking at the orchestra seated in front of a huge picture window with an incredible view of the Atlantic Ocean outside.

Visitors to the concert can watch waves crashing and lights twinkling on the water outside, which creates an evocative and memorable experience when listening to the music being played by this exceptional orchestra.

The Alfredo Kraus Auditorium was built as a beacon for opera, music and ballet in the Canary Islands. However, who was Alfredo Kraus?

Alfredo Kraus Trujillo was born in Las Palmas on 24 September 1927 - the son of a Spanish naturalised Austrian. Alfredo began piano lessons at the age of four and after completing secondary education he studied industrial engineering.

Soon after graduation, Kraus began to concentrate more and more on singing, which he studied in Barcelona, Madrid and later Italy.

Alfredo Kraus made his operatic debut as the Duke of Mantua in Giuseppe Verdi's Rigoletto in Cairo, in January 1956. He then appeared in La Traviata in Venice, Turin and London, and in 1958 made his first appearances in Rome and Lisbon.

Kraus quickly developed into a world class tenor, starred in a movie based on the life of Gayarre, an early famous Spanish tenor, and became a frequent and well-respected performer at the world's most prestigious opera houses, singing with Maria Callas, Joan Sutherland and other world-renowned sopranos.

The last two years of Kraus's life were darkened by the death of his wife in 1997, which affected him deeply. A proud and strong-willed man, he eventually returned to the stage and to teaching, making the comment, "Singing is a form of admitting that I'm alive."

In 1991, Kraus was awarded the Prince of Asturias Award. In 1997, his home city of Las Palmas opened the Alfredo Kraus Auditorium in his honour. Kraus died on September 10, 1999 in Madrid, at the age of 71, after a long illness.

The music of Strauss and Mahler soothed my ears and made me forget the world outside. I felt inspired by watching the professionals playing their violins, violas and cellos with such enthusiasm and grace. During my next practice sessions, I will try harder.

If you are visiting or live on the island, I strongly recommend a visit to the auditorium and, better still, to experience a concert given by the Gran Canaria Philharmonic Orchestra. Link this to a good meal in one of the many nearby restaurants, and I suspect that you too will have a most enjoyable evening that you will remember for a long time to come.

Wish You Were Here

When was the last time that you sent a postcard? I guess, if you are anything like most of the younger members of the population, it was some time ago; maybe several years. Thinking about this question recently, I realised that I haven't sent any for several years, but with the exception of one of those fun and expensive 3D picture postcards that we thought our elderly aunt would enjoy receiving. Sadly, she didn't even mention it when I spoke to her, so I doubt it made any impression, and we needn't have bothered.

It came as no surprise to read that the UK's foremost publisher of picture postcards, J Salmon is going to stop production in December. This family-owned company has been publishing calendars and postcards since 1880, but now sales have dried up.

Charles and Harry Salmon, the fifth generation of the family of postcard publishers, recently commented that the popularity of social media has had such a negative impact upon their business that their production was now unsustainable. Many will remember the beautiful scenic shots, the comic ones, as well as those very 'rude' ones that were often so popular at seaside beach shops.

I still like to receive postcards and pin them to a display board. It is fascinating to receive a card from some faraway place that I have never visited. A postcard from somewhere that I remember is also welcome, since it brings back many happy memories and experiences.

The closest that I get to this nowadays is sending a 'virtual postcard' to a few special people with one of my own photos, by using an app on my smartphone. It is quick, convenient and good value and takes away the need to try to find a post office in some foreign land to buy a stamp, only to find that it has closed for siesta.

Do you remember that well-worn phrase to quizzes in newspapers, magazines and radio shows? It was always "Answers on a postcard please"; now it is "send a text to…", usually at a premium rate charge. The demise of the humble postcard seems to have gone almost unnoticed.

As a replacement for postcards, many people now post some of the more ecstatic moments of their holiday experience on Facebook, Instagram and other social media sites. This is fine for the sender, but how many of us are bored senseless with seeing endless platefuls of holiday food from some exotic holiday destination on Facebook, and the alcoholic "I'm all hung over" posts that seem to have replaced the humble postcard from the younger generation.

Are today's electronic offerings intended as merely a showcase for the sender, or for the enjoyment of the receiver, I wonder? Do we really need to see yet another pizza or giant plateful of a cooked English breakfast? A shot of the Leaning Tower of Pisa or a pretty Venetian canal boat would be a nice alternative; just a thought.

A few years ago, I remember spending several enjoyable hours sorting through a battered suitcase belonging to a great aunt containing hundreds of sepia postcards with stamps bearing the head of long dead monarchs. Photographs of exotic destinations, such as Weymouth, Edinburgh, Yarmouth and Blackpool, peppered with occasional postcards from more adventurous destinations, such as Venice, Bruges and Paris. As well as the fascination of seeing how popular resorts have changed over the years, the comments on the back were often very revealing.

I remember some of the lengthy discussions that my parents had when selecting postcards for family members and friends when we were on a family holiday. Should we send a scenic shot of the beach to Aunt Joy, would Uncle Frank like something a little more cultured, or is that one just far too rude for cousin Paul? We had better be careful what we write on the back of that one to Brenda, because we know that her postman always reads them, and he is such a gossip...

I shall miss those photographic treasures from J Salmon and other publishers. I guess that the publishers are right to draw a halt to the production of this much-loved remnant of the past. Like so many things in our lives, times change and maybe it is now time that the humble postcard be relegated to history.

26319347R00112

Printed in Great Britain
by Amazon